THE DRAMA IN EUROPE
IN THEORY AND PRACTICE

ROMAN THEATRE, DOUGGA, NORTH AFRICA

THE
DRAMA IN EUROPE
IN THEORY AND PRACTICE

BY

ELEANOR F. JOURDAIN
M.A., OXON

DOCTOR OF THE UNIVERSITY OF PARIS; PRINCIPAL OF ST. HUGH'S COLLEGE, OXFORD;
SOMETIME TAYLORIAN LECTURER IN THE UNIVERSITY OF OXFORD

WITH A FRONTISPIECE AND DIAGRAM

HASKELL HOUSE PUBLISHERS Ltd.
Publishers of Scarce Scholarly Books
NEW YORK. N. Y. 10012
1972

HASKELL HOUSE PUBLISHERS Ltd.
Publishers of Scarce Scholarly Books
280 LAFAYETTE STREET
NEW YORK. N. Y. 10012

Library of Congress Cataloging in Publication Data

Jourdain, Eleanor Frances, 1863-1924.
    The drama in Europe in theory and practice.

    Reprint of the 1924 ed.
    Bibliography: p.
    1. Drama—History and criticism. 2. Theater—
History. I. Title.
PN1721.J67 1972   809.2'0094   72-3216
ISBN 0-8383-1497-X

PREFACE

THIS book is intended to be an introduction to a very large subject, but not an attempt to reduce the whole subject within the limits of a small volume. Hence the reader will find that some parts—the more important to the argument—are more fully developed than others, in which only suggestions for further study have been made. The illustrations are intentionally limited to those which can be afforded by a few well-known plays.

The object of the book is to be an aid to literary history and appreciation. It is hoped that the student of a special dramatic literature will be able to see the part taken by that literature in the general development of drama and of the staging of plays.

ELEANOR F. JOURDAIN

St. Hugh's College
Oxford
August, 1923

CONTENTS

LIST OF ILLUSTRATIONS

INTRODUCTION

THERE has been a tendency in books on the Æsthetic of the Drama to separate Æsthetic —the philosophy of the subject—from its art and craft, with the result that the study of stage technique has become increasingly a matter of habit and tradition, while the study of dramatic theory has been undertaken in connexion with the theory of the other fine arts, and a philosophy of the subject formulated, which tends to get out of touch with the facts of stage production.

The literary study of the drama does, however, necessarily induce the critic to be aware both of theory and practice ; and of their connexion, and reaction one upon another. For instance, a study of the setting of a play is a very important adjunct to the study of its literary expression and human meaning. The dramatist, at any given period, writes with a knowledge of theatrical conditions, and at the same time he determines—in theory at any rate— whether his aim is to abide by or to modify these conditions. Thus, the provision for scenery, either solid or movable, has proved at different times to be a limitation or an opportunity to the dramatist, having regard to the particular aim of his work. The structure of the Athenian stage, intimately connected with the religious and social aim of the drama, its national appeal and moral lesson, was one which while suitable to the great periods of Greek drama, needed considerable modification at a later period, and would have been unsuitable for the plays of greater complexity and more limited appeal of our modern world. The solid " sets " of the Italian stage of the sixteenth and seventeenth centuries were the nearest thing to the representation of Italian " al fresco " life, in a country in which the chief incidents of a plot could be expected to happen in the open air : but they were not compatible with the change of scenery desired in the Romantic drama.

Attention to these and other conditions of stage technique brings out the fact that in all periods known as " classical," whether in Greece or Rome, in the seventeenth or eighteenth centuries in France or England, the drama has frequently been adapted to an existing stage technique. At all periods where plays of romance and adventure have been the dominant type, there have been efforts to adapt and modify the stage to the play. Thus the art of the classic dramatist makes use of symbols : the romantic writer tries for realism. Both attempt to liberate and expand the imagination, though in different ways.

In the first case we see on the stage a representation of life that is compressed in presentation by the necessity of the facts. The stage is less than the dramatist's world : the actors cannot compass a whole " comédie humaine," and representation has to be enhanced to produce the desired effect. Because the expression must be incomplete it is translated into symbols that are emphatic and significant : and thus the idea of life presented by the dramatist, while limited by its production in space and time, is unlimited in its effect on the imagination.

So in the Elizabethan drama a group of two or three men in *Henry V* may represent an army, or part of an army, but they are chosen to express distinct types and thus give an impression of complexity. In the French classical drama the army does not appear, but a herald explains that the army is at hand, and leaves the rest to the imagination. It is poor criticism to say that Shakespeare's types are exaggerated : he could give the impression of complexity in no other way but by emphasis on difference. In modern musical comedy the size of an army or navy is often suggested, as in *Pinafore*, by a few people almost exactly alike. But then the authors were concerned with expressing not the complex life of the nation but its mechanical and humorous aspect.

Again, it is poor criticism to ask—though Voltaire in the eighteenth century did ask—why only a herald should appear in a French classical play and leave the army to the imagination. In the theory of the French classical drama the importance of a crowd or army is the vital stimulus it produces. This is implied by the excitement of the herald's description of events ; and the effect is heightened by the fear and the mystery suggested by the unseen host in the background.[1]

Now the elements of the presentation of the play, its emphatic elements above all, can either be selected for their simplicity (and this is the case with primitive

---

[1] The need for emphasis of some kind explains the gorgeousness of dress in the Elizabethan play, allied to the sobriety of staging, and explains the significant gestures and tones in the French drama by which the play of passions on the stage is communicated to the audience. It explains, too, in the Japanese theatre (in the historic No series) the archaic and exaggerated dress, and the extremely slow *tempo* of the play ; the long-drawn gestures and slow wailing words. Or to go back to the origins of Western drama, it explains in part the fixed masks and the cothurnus of the Greek tragedy.

folk-drama everywhere, and with all art that tends
to the expression of pure feeling, as with the art of
the *dr.ame* of the eighteenth century in France, or with
that of the Romantic drama [1]) or these elements can
be selected in reference to a dominating idea. This
is the case in drama which makes more than a primitive
appeal ; and selection according to a dominant idea
produces style in representation. [2]

The need for emphasis is, however, balanced by
another need. This is for empty, neutral space which
shall satisfy the desire for a representation of great
distances and foreign lands and which shall be capable
of a sudden transformation from one atmosphere or
poetic district into another. Thus the sixteenth-
century French play of Hardy's, representing at once
action on the Tigris and the Euphrates, was only
possible where the few narrow boards on trestles were
unencumbered with stage furniture. The sixteenth-
century English stage had doors which might lead to
" Asia " on the one side and " Africa " on the other. [3]

[1] As for instance in de Musset's " Théâtre."

[2] When a Pierrot play was acted by some French students
at Sèvres they seized on the main idea that the life of a
pierrot is only half life, and the moonlight scenes are an expression of this. Their scenery was selected according to this
idea. Everything—trees, background, houses, costumes—
were designed in black and white. Everything was represented bleached by the drenching moonlight ; colour and
full-blooded life were absent. Pierrot's moment was the
moonlit dream.

[3] See the allusion in Sir Philip Sidney's *Apology*, 1596,
but written earlier, in which he questions the wisdom of
this appeal to the imagination, and prefers the Aristotelian
unities. " For where the stage should alwaies represent
but one place, and the uttermost time presupposed in it
should be, both by *Aristoteles* precept and common reason,
but one day, there is both many days and many places.
unartificially imagined. But if it be so in *Gorboduck* how
much more in all the rest, where you shall have *Asia* of the

The neutral ground between was the setting for romance. The sixteenth-century Italian play used the piazza for such scenes, and in Italy does not everything happen in a piazza? It belongs to every one and to no one. An empty space, neutral in its content, is as necessary to a play as the emphatic dress or gesture or words that are intended to strike the imagination and people the scene with mysterious events.

In many forms of drama this creation of an atmosphere of expectation in a quiet and neutral place is supposed to be engineered by supernatural forces.[1] This is again only a different way of producing an impression on the audience. Macbeth's witches on the desolate heath make the future alive with fear. The ghost of Thyestes in Seneca's *Agamemnon* produces by his recital the certainty of the horror that is to oppress his descendants, and he calls up his son—invisible to the audience, though (later) one of the living characters of the play—to hear what is in store for him, and he addresses the last lines of the speech to Ægisthus, as if he were actually present.[2]

It is the neutral space in the centre of the stage

one side, and *Affrick* of the other, and so many other under-Kingdoms, that the Player, when he commeth in, must ever begin with telling you where he is, or els, the tale will not be conceived."

[1] The Greek play begins with the offering of incense on the altar, and thus produces the effect of a relation with unknown forces.

[2] Seneca always has the sense of the stage value of his methods, and he makes free use of every thrilling incident. Such a piece of stage art as the speech of the ghost of Thyestes, only bearable at a moment of great emotion, is founded on Seneca's own conception of the attitude of the spirit returning to earth. "I come sent forth from Tartarus' deep pit, doubting which world I hate the more. Thyestes flees the lower, the upper he puts to flight." In all Seneca's tragedies the spirit is ready to terrify the human being to whom he appears.

that is used for the creation of atmosphere in tragedy. In comedy it is the place where the strands of the plot are knitted together and finally unravelled. What happens behind the scenes is engineered by what happens on the stage. The drama of jealousy or madness is played out in the minds of the actors and is visible to the spectator. Behind the scene, in the Greek play, the inevitable consequences are worked out ; and by the time they are in train they are recognized to be inevitable.

The main necessity for a " classical " play in a theatre, however primitive, is material for symbolic representation which shall emphasize the important elements in the play ; and the existence of a space which may be anywhere and represent any period, or any succession of places and periods, within which the dramatic presentation of significant words, gestures and events may take place.

On the other hand, the romantic or adventurous play leads to an attempt to appeal through the gates of the ear and eye to the imagination. Change of place—itself a stimulus to the imagination—is suggested by a change of scenery. The scenery itself is no longer symbolic but is pictorial. It becomes archæologically correct, or, at the least, likely. Music may enter into the action, while providing at the same time an atmosphere within which anything may happen. In the Romantic drama of the nineteenth century we see the suggested expansion of time and space instead of its limitation. The plays of de Musset have very varied backgrounds, those of Hugo a considerable list of incidents. Both carry the audience away from common experience ; both require costume and scenery to produce an effect of reality which would otherwise be insufficiently supported.

A further problem which enters into questions of literary criticism is that of the relation of the audience to the events on the stage. In " classical " plays of whatever country, the effect aimed at by both writers of tragedy and comedy is that of contrast with ordinary daily life. Heroes, as in Corneille, are of superhuman moral quality; villains, as in Crébillon and Voltaire, are deeply dyed. Absurd and vicious characters, as in Molière and Regnard, have their faults more clearly delineated than would be usual in a picture of life as it actually is. The experience of life of Hamlet, of Lady Macbeth, of Lear and Cordelia is deeply cut, and unlike the usual human story, though it possesses a full human appeal. With the advent of the democratic element into social life before the French Revolution, this theory of stage production changed; and the dramatist attempted to claim the sympathy of the audience for a life on the stage that was interesting because so like ordinary life, and not contrasted with it. Lying between a great period of classic and a great period of Romantic literature in France and other European countries there is the eighteenth-century *drame* which fulfils the condition of assimilating life on the stage to life as it was seen and lived.

A dramatist has then to ask himself whether he aims at a close relation between the stage and life, or at remoteness and effects of contrast. The structure of the European stage has here followed the lines marked out by the dramatic writer. The problem did not become acute in Greece, for the flow of emotion could be directed one way or another by the will of the author. The chorus in a Greek play belongs at times to the audience whom it addresses, or to the actors whom it exhorts, or to invisible and watching spectators whom it represents. The problem appears, however, in all drama later than that of classical Greece, and is resolved in different ways according to the tendency of the drama to appeal by contrast or by similarity of experience ; and according to the different ways, classic or romantic, in which contrast may be produced.   That is, either by the delineation of acute psychological experience in the minds of the characters, as in Racine's tragedies or in Ibsen's plays, or by an imaginative treatment of the effect of widened experience on their natures, as in Shakespeare's comedies, the Spanish drama of the sixteenth or seventeenth centuries, or in nine-teenth-century Romantic drama.[1]

The stage has evidently meant something very different at different periods when the parts of the actors, the staging, and the moral meaning of the play have been so greatly transformed.   In ancient Greece the representation of a play had the character of a religious and national ceremony, and its interest was bound to be general and even universal.   After the classical revival in the sixteenth and seventeenth centuries, tragedy became a means of expressing the human nature and human character of the time and nation in question : its importance was more ephemeral. Where realism is apparent, as in countries affected by the Elizabethan tradition, the setting acquires importance.   Where, as in the Latin countries, the play of mind is more important than its symbolic representation, scenery and staging are reduced to the minimum.   It is perhaps not too much to say

[1] A close relation between the stage and life was not used as an ideal of stage-production till the eighteenth century.   It is true that in Elizabethan drama the actors spoke from an " apron " or proscenium projecting into the space filled by the audience : an actor could make his exit through the crowd.   But the physical contact thus obtained was counteracted by dress and gesture that was frankly more striking than the dress and gesture of ordinary life.

that while Shakespeare and Racine offer us remarkable instances of these two different kinds of treatment, there are plays and moments in the plays, when Æschylus and Sophocles show the double tendency of the stage combined in a degree which the moderns have not yet reached. For the moderns have tended either to complexity of setting or to complexity of plot, and no one has attempted the complete fusion of the two. In fact, the fusion has only occurred in drama such as that of ancient Greece, in which the whole of human life is regarded as subject to a fate, either called down by one of the principal characters or implicit in the general atmosphere of the play. The revival of dramatic art in the Middle Ages under conditions of thought which brought with them a belief in the free-will and free action of man, released the drama from the fate-motive, but inevitably produced disintegration of form and complexity of subject-matter. The æsthetic problem involved has only been dealt with in general terms by great dramatists such as Shakespeare and Racine who instinctively recognized the force of fate as a motive in primitive drama, and the possibility of a development in the play of characters which have acquired liberty in the Christian sense.

Other forms of drama were produced by men who, like Marie-Joseph Chénier, put another strong motive (as for example that of love of country) in the place of the classical fate-motive.

The relation of such theories of the drama to stage-production is the object of this study.

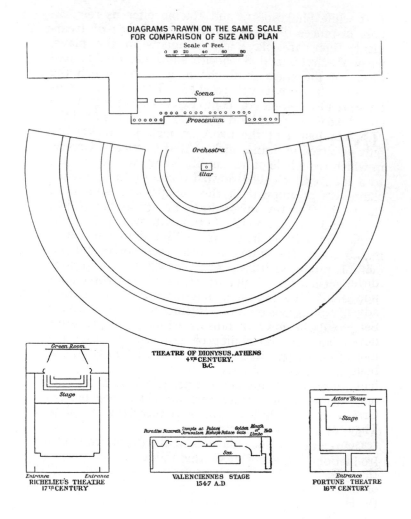

DIAGRAMS DRAWN ON THE SAME SCALE
FOR COMPARISON OF SIZE AND PLAN

Scale of Feet

0 10 20   40   60   80

Scena

Proscenium

Orchestra

Altar

THEATRE OF DIONYSUS, ATHENS
4ᵀᴴ CENTURY.
B.C.

Green Room

Stage

Entrance *Entrance*
RICHELIEU'S THEATRE
17ᵀᴴ CENTURY

Paradise *Nazareth* *Temple at* *Palace* *Golden* *Mouth*
          Jerusalem *Bishops* *Palace* *Gate* *of*
                      Palace   *Limbo* *Hell*

Sea

VALENCIENNES STAGE
154·7 A.D

Actors' House

Stage

Entrance
FORTUNE THEATRE
16ᵀᴴ CENTURY

THE DRAMA IN EUROPE
IN THEORY AND PRACTICE

CHAPTER I

GREEK AND ROMAN PLAYS

ANCIENT Greece produced an art in which the characters of freedom and of order were both evident. The country itself had a developed political life, its city-states, neither large nor small: its people had a taste for voyages and adventures, a great love for liberty and good laws. Set in a part of the peninsula where civilization had developed in a better climate, and in circumstances more favourable than those of its immediate neighbours, whether on the islands or the mainlands, Greece had an ideal to maintain, and this could be done only by the strictest attention to order in life The Greeks were afraid of chaos, moral and political. They dreaded letting primitive emotion overwhelm reason. They cultivated a certain detachment from people living grosser lives and having lower tastes than their own. They had raised themselves out of the " slime " [1] of the Pelasgians, and had become the Hellenes, who would fight equally for moral integrity and political liberty.

[1] See Gilbert Murray, *Four Stages of Greek Religion.*

The art of ancient Greece reflected its life. It described and portrayed with great sanity and freedom the acts of a life that was being lived with zest. Great artists were accustomed to treat all human experience as material for art, even the experience which in modern eyes is relatively earthly and sensual. They had a very large scope, and a considerable store of courage. They treated their gods with interest and familiarity, and gave to their images certain definite characteristics. The artist never failed to give a form to his idea, and he made both form and idea true to fact: the one to the fact of nature, the other to the fact of imagination. The appeal he made, then, is one that we feel now, because it touches something so deeply imbedded in human nature as to be of its essence.[1]

The Greeks had a sense of a social and religious ideal which made the national gatherings in the theatre a real part of the national life. East of Ionia and the islands there is no such development of human society and art.[2]

The drama, having its origin in a communal gathering, with harvest revels and ancestor-worship as the

[1] Greece in the fifth century felt the need for an enduring art. It was a time of great and fruitful national activity—and her statues, her philosophy and her drama all witness to her desire to perpetuate the glory of her people, and what was better, to leave behind her a pattern and example of an art which was so beautifully ordered and proportioned that it has never fallen out of a true perspective or lost its force, as a more meretricious art would have done.

See Racine, Preface to *Iphigénie*.

[2] This ideal still persists in Greece, where the annual revels take place on the threshing-floor of each village, and plays are still acted in the ancient theatres. See Ridgeway, *Origin of Tragedy*, and the confirmatory evidence of other travellers; also Dörpfeld und Reisch, *Das Griechische Theater*, etc., p. 368.

central impulse to give form to the rejoicings, had at first a fixed form or ritual in which certain traditional elements recur : e.g. in comedy a marriage, a feast, a dispute, a reconciliation ; in tragedy a vow, the working out of family history, the Nemesis, the sacrifice. Attendance at these plays was an act of traditional piety and a pledge of present citizenship. The theatre was, in a real sense, a democratic institution ; and the building of the fixed theatres emphasized the fact.[1]

In the course of time traditional stories became subject to variation. After Æschylus and Sophocles there came a change. Euripides treated the life-history of an individual showing how he emerged as a person from the forces of his race and time, took up his own burden, and made himself master of his fate within the limits imposed by the laws of humanity.

A Greek play was intended to appeal to a very large mass of people who came—much in the spirit in which people have attended the Passion Play at Oberammergau or the Wagnerian play-cycles at Bayreuth and at Munich—to give themselves up to a performance lasting over several days ; one, too, of which the intensity had a religious character. Hence two requisites became very important : a *theatre* or place for seeing, capable of seating a large number of spectators, and a method of staging a play that would convey to a large number of people across a considerable distance the meaning of a definite plot and action, through words and also through gesture and· attitude and through rhythmical movement.

Thus it follows that the large and simple Greek

[1] The stone theatres in Greece were mainly constructed in the fourth century B.C., thus later than the great productions of the classic drama. See Dörpfeld und Reisch, *Das Griechische Theater*, etc.

stage was the field for the working out of a plot which contained a very few characters, the traits of which were vividly brought out. This at once differentiates a Greek play from a mediæval or modern one in which additional minor characters can be constantly brought in and the scene can be continually changed. Plot and characterization in a Greek play depend intimately on one another. This is not necessarily the case on the modern stage, where we sometimes have a plot elaborately worked out, together with little development in the characters. For example, Molière's *L'Avare* is a character-study allied to a plot which is obvious rather than ingenious. Regnard's *Le Légataire Universel*, on the other hand, has a well-constructed plot but little or no development of character. The comedy of the Restoration in England and the " well-constructed " plays of Scribe and Augier in France are examples of excellent plot construction, while the characters are conventional types.

But the best plays in the Greek tragic drama show a high skill in construction and the characters are few and finely developed by interaction one with another. In studying Greek drama we are then well aware of the conditions and limitations of the stage which render simplicity and force in the play the main conditions of success. The beauty of a Greek play —it has been said—emerges from a sustained struggle with the difficulties of its production.

In its origins, Greek drama, whether tragic or comic, was developed from very primitive and uncomplicated material. It is now generally agreed that the tragic play developed from the action of a chorus, engaged in singing or recitation in honour of the god Dionysus, or, as Ridgeway has inferred, in honour of a dead hero (whence the introduction of a tomb on the stage). The comic play, also arising from Dionysiac celebrations, took note of the changing seasons, with their appropriate celebrations. The threshing-floor was the original orchestra or dancing-place. In tragedy the altar to the god is always present; in comedy, as Cornford shows,[1] we have the regular recurrence of certain incidents, notably the marriage-feast, in every play, even in the late satirical comedy of Aristophanes, and this points to a primitive origin in the cult of the life-process.

The fact that the chorus was originally called the chorus of satyrs, companions of the wandering god, Dionysus, is also significant of the origins of the drama.

In Athens in the fifth century B.C. we can trace these survivals of the primitive idea, but the chorus has developed a leader who has a spoken dialogue with a character outside the chorus, and who is known as the actor.[2] The leader also harangues the rest of the chorus—and like all mob orators finds a stone or wooden platform on which to stand when he addresses the rest of the chorus, though when he is himself part of the chorus he stands on the same level as the others.

Æschylus is said to have introduced a second actor: the two actors taking each, if necessary, more than one part. Thus the elements of dramatic action were produced.[3]

Sophocles added a third " actor " and raised the number of the chorus from twelve to fifteen.[4]

[1] Cornford, *The Origin of Attic Comedy.*
[2] Village dances in Greece still have a leader, who dances differently from the rest.
[3] See Aristotle, *Poetics*, IV. 13 (written about 330 B.C.): " Æschylus first introduced a second actor: he diminished the importance of the chorus, and assigned the leading parts to the dialogue."
[4] See *Poetics*, 10–15. He is said also to have introduced scene-painting. See, on this point, Bywater, *Aristotle's Poetics*, and Lessing, *Leben Sophokles.*

To meet the need for a suitable presentation of drama, theatres were hollowed out in hill-sides, and tiers of seats arranged. The flat central space or orchestra [1] (corresponding to the dancing-place or threshing-floor), and containing the altar to the god, was the place where, originally, the action of the play developed. The chorus were given symmetrically opposite entrances, one on each side of the space where the circular rows of seats were cut, and where eventually was placed the *proscenium, logeion,* or speaking-place, behind which was the *skene, scena,* or booth, where the actors dressed: the front wall of which served as background to the play.[2] In some theatres (not in that of Athens) an underground passage led from stage buildings to orchestra.

There is considerable controversy about the time at which the *scena* and the *proscenium* became the places from which the actors spoke, instead of from the orchestra. But when the change occurred, or even earlier, some kind of painting on the wall behind the *logeion* became customary, and on it was depicted a palace or a temple, with columns and doors. Aristotle says that the change occurred in the time of Sophocles.[3]

When the change took place, the actors who were intended to represent characters closely connected with the action came in at one side, and those who

[1] Paved in lozenge-shaped pattern under the altar.

[2] The original meaning of the word *proskenion* was the wall in front of the *skene,* and that wall (at first of wood) was a background to the action in the *orchestra.*

[3] See footnote [4] on preceding page. Possibly the sacrificial platform behind the altar was the earliest raised place on which an actor could detach himself from the chorus. In the plays of Euripides the actors speak from the roof of the *proskenion* (about 10 feet above the orchestra) and the gods appear above it again. See J. T. Allen, *The Greek Theater of the Fifth Century before Christ.*

were supposed to arrive from different countries came in at the other. Changes of scene were rare: there were only two in the classical tragedies we know; and the effect was then produced by revolving prisms, or *periaktoi*.[1]

One of the earliest examples of this kind of theatre is the theatre of Dionysus at Athens. Enough remains of it still to show pretty clearly its ancient construction. It was calculated to hold at least 20,000 people, and Plato, in the *Symposium*, says that it held on occasion many more spectators. The girth of the great amphitheatre is about four times as great as that of the largest opera-house in London—Covent Garden—but its circular shape makes it the best possible theatre for sound. The theatre of Athens is also about four times as wide as the large " Salle Richelieu " used for the more elaborate plays in Paris during the seventeenth and eighteenth centuries, or as the opera-houses at Versailles or Bayreuth.[2]

The Greek theatre was of necessity an outdoor and open-air theatre : the only shelter being that provided for the actors. It was so cut in the side of a hill that beyond the columns and flat roof of the actors' building could be seen trees and sky, and often the line of hills, as at Delphi, or the line of the sea, as at Syracuse and Athens. There was thus an element of natural though distant scenery, something, too, normal and habitual about the hill-side and its surroundings which gave a real background to the play, though one so large as to be symbolic of nature as a whole rather than of any particular aspect of nature.

Against the play of life in the upper air and clouds,

[1] Platforms on rollers sometimes came in containing a tableau of the facts enacted behind the scenes.

[2] See, for illustration of this point, the diagrams drawn to scale (frontispiece).

made real to the spectator by the moving breeze,
against the glittering line of the sea, or the swelling
outline of the hills, a story of " a certain magnitude,"
as Aristotle called it, was being acted that represented
some perennial problem of human life, and was in
its outlines true to its surroundings in the past, and
would be true and significant for years to come.

Acting and staging had to be on an heroic scale to
compete with real scenery and combine with it. The
problem had to be acute and the action important
and perhaps impersonal in its issues. There were no
star parts on a Greek stage : nor did an actor " create "
a part as he does on the modern stage, though he might
become identified with it.

The actors had to be unduly tall, to give the necessary emphasis to their rôle. Their expressions had
to be fixed by a mask to give the necessary meaning
and coherence to their parts. It is often noticed
that scenes of violence and of murder did not take
place on the stage itself, and the reticence and restraint
of Greek art is often quoted as the cause. But it
may be noticed that masks, and high boots producing
the effect of stilts, made physical violence on the stage
all but impossible. There was, therefore, a practical
as well as an æsthetic reason for the conduct and
form/of the play. Movements had to be statuesque
in order to give the necessary effect of repose, and
also of significance, to the audience at a distance.
The whole play had to be staged with emphasis and
at a slow *tempo* to be effective against the background
and to be telling in its appeal. Variety of *tempo*
and contrast were produced by the rhythmical movements of the chorus, which we can imagine with
some security since the different lyrical metres used
were translated into movement. Rhythm can express
every grade of feeling, and the measures in the parts

given to the chorus in Sophocles' *Œdipus Tyrannus* will give an idea of the illustrative variety of the choric movement.

Greek tragedy possessed in its chorus an enveloping musical atmosphere, and this atmosphere must therefore have been implicit in the original idea of tragedy which developed from the chorus.[1] The significance of this fact lies partly in the power which music possesses of suggesting a unity of emotion which has not yet perhaps achieved expression in words or gesture, partly in the power which music undoubtedly possesses of recalling emotion in the past, or of producing sensations such as those of awe, hope, or fear, with which the future may be regarded. Greek tragedy, far from being only an intellectual conflict, is an experience of the whole nature of man, including his emotional side, and thus makes use of musical rhythm and tone. The world in which the members of a Greek chorus live and act, has this, too, in common with the world of music, that it is one in which anything may happen, according to the will of the author. The chorus has a superhuman knowledge of events in the past and present : it has prophetic knowledge of the future. It represents detached views on the nature of the tragic conflict.[2]

[1] A flute-player accompanied the chorus in the Greek play : and the Roman play continued this tradition.

[2] See, on this point, Bethe, *Prolegomena*, etc., and Nietzsche, *The Birth of Tragedy*. A similar deduction can be made from the words and acts of the chorus in the Comedies. Here the chorus often represents the undisciplined and primitive element in life, and also the element that possesses the intuitive knowledge which often paralyses action, and thus the actors, ignorant of coming events, plunge in and out of complications to which the chorus possesses the key. Menander's chorus of drunken youths expresses ironically " in vino veritas."

While the chorus could act and move rhythmically and deploy in front of the actors, the actors, observed on all three sides, could do little but move into position, speak their parts, and move out again. The chorus then incidentally prevented any great movement on the part of the actors.[1] Euripides, however, made the chorus a free lyric, and thus its influence was not necessarily identified with the action. In some plays, such as the *Medea*, *Iphigenia in Tauris*, and the *Ion*, the chorus is detached, and shows this by its sympathy with Medea, its interference with the plot in the other two plays. In other plays, such as the *Helena*, the *Iphigenia*, and the *Phœnissæ*, the chorus consists of women who are foreigners by race. In Euripides' individual conception of drama the chorus was material, to be used or dispensed with as he chose. The musical phrases used in Euripides' choric odes were made to fit the corresponding poetic phrases, and thus, both in form and content, the chorus served as an interval between the scenes.

Euripides, too, recognized the advantages of a prologue, which should describe and define the characters to come on during the play.[2]

In two other ways Euripides instituted a new tradition in the Attic theatre. In his *Electra* he tried the experiment of using the background of a peasant's life for the tragedy of the central character. These simple scenes served to throw up the main action and also to give it a natural and human character. He also made frequent use of a device for concluding the play by bringing in a deity to mark the relation between the story and the gods who control the issues

---

[1] The priests and archons were in front of the people, and made a boundary between the audience and the play.

[2] This method was parodied by Shakespeare in the Clowns' play in *A Midsummer Night's Dream*.

of life and death. Sometimes, as in the *Bacchæ*, the god appears at the beginning of the play as well as at the end, and his influence is felt all through it. In connexion with this method of Euripides' art, two platforms were arranged on the stage of his day, one giving the effect of a throne for place-deities such as Apollo—and another lifted high above the actors' house, and served by pulleys, a crane or " μηχανή," in which gods from the upper air appear : this is the origin of the expression, the " Deus ex machina." We find the effect of a realistic entry of superhuman powers in the *Hippolytus*, the *Bacchæ*, the *Andromache*, and *Orestes*.[1]

A late change in the chorus was the appearance of the *Parabasis* or author's speech : when the chorus all faced the audience and the leader spoke as the author, giving an account of his aims in the play.

In Greek tragedy the theme was always well known : this was a very natural concession to the needs of a large audience which, unprovided with a book of the words, could gather from the title the necessary historical course of the play, and could be free to watch for anything striking or interesting in the method of treatment. French dramatic art, from the sixteenth to the eighteenth century, adopted a similar method. Most young authors attempted an *Œdipus* early—as did Corneille and Voltaire—and we find seventeen versions of the story of Sophonisba within the space of 200 years. In England in the age of Dryden the same plan was pursued. Later, towards the end of the eighteenth century, classical story

---

[1] In the *Clouds*, by Aristophanes, provision is made for letting Socrates down by a crane from the house-roof to the orchestra, and other examples may be found in the same author.

retired to the Opera, where, enriched by music and spectacular effects, the stories of Orpheus and of Iphigenia were re-told with a new glory, and became the material of a new art.

The setting of comedy in a Greek theatre differed in certain ways from that of tragedy : notably in the size of the chorus, which was twenty-four instead of twelve or fifteen. We notice in modern musical comedy the tendency for the chorus to outbalance the actors, and this was, too, the case in ancient Greece. It has been possible to discover the number of the chorus in Aristophanes from the *Birds*, where the birds are named as they come on. The effect produced is meant to be grotesque, or at the least striking, as in the *Clouds*, the *Wasps*, and the *Acharnians*.[1]

Jests in comedy were apt to be local in their origin and application. (This is of course also true of the comedy of Shakespeare and Molière.) The epilogue of the Westminster play is a modern survival of the punning habit which put the audience into good tune in ancient Greece.

Greek comedy produced a surprise in the way of a plot, and well-marked types, instead of carefully-drawn and developing studies of character. Great attention was paid to by-play : for while in the comedies of Aristophanes as many as four actors appeared on the stage, the tradition (as reported by Horace) was that only three of them took part in the dialogue. A silent actor was frequently present, who helped the action by dumb show. In Aristophanes' plays, too, there is an occasional dialogue between an actor and a member of the chorus. The

[1] Where the conscientious objectors form the chorus.

effect was to increase the vivacity of the representation.[1]

The " new comedy " of Menander, reflecting, as it did, a more corrupt age than that of Aristophanes, depended more on realistic presentation of the detail of life than did the " old comedy." But though not inferior in skill of construction and presentation, and more in touch with actual social conditions, the comedy of Menander has less spring and force than that of Aristophanes.[2]

The chorus was retained by Menander, as a concession to popular tradition, with much the same meaning as it had borne in Aristophanes. That is, the indication " chorus " merely meant a lyrical interlude, which served as a division between the acts of a play. Where, however, the chorus took any part in the action, the words of the dialogue were put in at length. It was only on rare occasions that the chorus in Menander exchanged a word with the actors.

Both actors and chorus moved on and off the stage in the New comedy : leaving the boards empty for a pause in the middle of the play.[3] The allusions in Menander make it clear that the background of the stage consisted of two houses, each with its entrance, in front of which the action took place. In certain comedies (for example in the fragment known as the

---

[1] The satyric play, which prevailed in Greece at the same time as comedy and tragedy (since we hear of the classical dramatists writing satyric plays), originated in the satyric chorus, from which also tragedy had developed. But it remained a rougher, more popular representation, and appealed by its unrestrained dancing and the coarseness of its allusions.

[2] The same phenomenon repeated itself in France in the eighteenth century, where great attention was paid to the setting of comedies which were, however, much inferior to those of Molière.

[3] See Rudolf Graf, *Szenische Untersuchungen zu Menander*.

Litigants) one house only was used. This practice of the Greek stage was repeated by Plautus and Terence in the versions in which they made use of the " new comedy."

Towards the third century B.C. Greek influence began to affect Roman ideas of art. From 332 B.C., when a Greek general, Alexander of Epirus, came to Italy to defend the men of Tarentum against the Samnites, an increasingly close contact was established between Italy and Greece, till when Rome aided Greece to obtain her freedom in 196 B.C., Plautus had already begun to write plays which departed from the rough popular comedy of local life, with its mixture of revelry, punning and satire, and to adapt Greek plots for a Roman audience, thus imposing a form on the dramatic sense of the period. In this Livius Andronicus, though still using the old Saturnian metre, had been a pioneer. His tragedies, the titles only of which are extant, were formed mainly on the Trojan theme. Nævius had the same sympathies, but also wrote plays on contemporary events. His comedies are more distinctively Roman than his tragedies. Up to the time of Plautus the Roman theatre consisted of a rough wooden stage with structures on it, and the spectators sat or stood on the sloped ground rising round it. Seats were added after 145 B.C., and in 55 B.C. the first stone theatre was built.

The Roman art of the stage was a development of the Greek. The Romans filled up the orchestra with seats, producing what we now call stalls, and in these sat the Senators. Since the crowd stood and made itself heard and felt on the slopes above, the actors had to appeal very plainly and forcibly to a mixed and mainly uneducated audience. A high wall was built up round the theatre, covered passages or corridors were made to connect stage and auditorium, scenery became more elaborate and shut out the world outside (the effect of this can be studied in the theatre at Orange). Certain conventions in dress were adopted [1] (such as the use of white wigs to denote age, black for youth, red for the slave class), which had the effect of making the meaning of the play and the character of the personages clear to the audience.

Vitruvius, a contemporary authority,[2] mentions decorated " scenes " of three kinds which were used on the Roman stage :

(1) Façades with columns, representing public buildings (for use in Tragedy).

(2) Private houses, with windows and balconies (for use in Comedy).

(3) Rustic scenes for the Satyric drama.[3]

The stage was long and narrow, and lent itself to variety of action. The exit to the actors' right symbolized the road to a town, that to the left the road to the country or the sea. Curtains were spread to shade from the sun and protect from rain, and the tiers of seats were made steep to afford further protection from the weather.[4]

[1] Some of which had been used in Greece.

[2] *De Architectura.*

[3] " There are three kinds of scenes : one called the tragic ; second, the comic ; third, the satyric. Their decorations are different and unlike each other in scheme. Tragic scenes are delineated with columns, pediments, statues, and other objects suited to kings ; comic scenes exhibit private dwellings, · with balconies and views representing rows of windows, after the manner of ordinary dwellings ; satyric scenes are decorated with trees, caverns, mountains, and other rustic objects, delineated in landscape style." Vitruvius, *De Architectura,* Book V, Ch. 6 (translated).

[4] The Sheldonian Theatre at Oxford is an almost perfect modern reproduction of the form of a Roman theatre, even to the roof, painted to imitate curtains and the ropes that drew them.

The plays of Plautus and Terence were written to be acted on the Roman stage, and bear a strict relation to its conditions. Thus dress, gesture and make-up supplied on the Roman stage a good deal of information about the characters, which in a more literary type of play is suggested in the dialogue. Thus, too, the avowed object of amusing the audience accounts for the way in which the play is often broken up into farcical elements. In spite of the flaws in construction, due to this desire to amuse at all hazards, Plautus produced a large gallery both of characters and of caricatures, and a series of situations which have served as models for the comic stage of later centuries.

As distinguished from the " old comedy " of Greece, the comedy of Plautus dispensed with a chorus, which had already begun to disappear both from tragedy and comedy in the later Greek period.[1] The form of the Roman theatre witnesses to the change, as no room is left for a chorus to deploy in the orchestra, now filled with seats. Variety was obtained in a different way on the Roman stage, for the dialogues between the characters were supplemented by *cantica* or monologues set to music. Here Plautus used a great variety of metres to express different emotional values. The metre changed appropriately with the mood of the actor and his relation to other actors or the audience. When the audience was taken into confidence a change of metre marked the moment.

Terence represented a revival of a more cultivated type of play, more polished in language and Greek in form. His plays differed from those of Plautus by being more complex in plot (he levied contributions from two or more Greek stories and bound them in one play), and by conveying, too, a deliberate theme

[1] See Bethe, *Prolegomena zur geschichte des Theaters in Alterthum*.

or intention which removes his plays from the category of those only intended to amuse an audience. Terence expressed, as Molière did in a later period, the revolt of youth against age, and the desire of all men to find a reason for conduct rather than to be guided by habit. His plays mark a transition to the literary play which departs from the stage and its limitations and becomes a comment on the manners of a restricted society. Such plays frequently read better than they act. But Terence's plays act well, though the expression and the form are literary. They furnished a large part of the training for colloquial and dramatic Latin in the schools of the Middle Ages.

Tragedy on the Roman stage was more traditional in character than was comedy. It possessed that background of general feeling and experience which was essential to a play in a Greek national theatre, and it dealt with problems which had a general human significance. But the typically Greek tragedy of Æschylus and Sophocles could not be re-stated in a form which would make an appeal to Rome as it had done to Athens: and the Roman tragedians were inclined to take their subjects from Euripides, who had himself broken away from the strict tradition of the Greek stage. Under the Roman Republic the stage became a means of cultivation and a school of rhetoric.

In Roman tragedy, though not in comedy, the chorus of the Greek play was retained. But instead of being a constant quantity in the action, the Roman chorus comes and goes. It fulfils the function of the servants in Elizabethan or French classical tragedy who come in as necessity arises and then withdraw when they are no longer needed.

In tragedy later than that of the Augustan Age the chorus proper disappeared from the play and

2

was replaced by lyric. On the Roman stage of this later period the " cantica " or lyric portions of the text were recited by a singer standing with a flute-player by the side of the stage while the actor used gesture to illustrate the words. In the tragedies of Seneca the Younger the chorus was unconnected with the action, and expressed the philosophic reflection of the author.

The tragedies of Seneca were written in the reign of Nero. They were probably not intended for stage presentation, but lent themselves to declamation, an art in which a rich and solid background rather than any definite scenery, or change of scenery, is indicated. The onus of the emotional effect falls on the one speaker. We cannot quote Seneca's tragedies as evidence in any matter of dramatic technique, but they have had so much influence on the art of France and Italy, England and Germany (curiously enough, not at all on Spain, which was Seneca's country, as he was born at Cordova), that it is worth while to consider what arrangement of plot Seneca had in his mind.

We have already seen that he made considerable use of the supernatural element to produce effects of terror, and also of remoteness from ordinary life, but he used this emphasis on terror as an artistic relief to a sensitive mind at a period of political terrorism. It is worth notice that Racine, where he is influenced by Seneca, as in *Bérénice*, is struck by exactly the same circumstances of social life as those which Seneca felt : that is by the corrupt and immoral lives of people in whose hands lay the political responsibility for the country, and the consequent reign of terror among the helpless and non-influential sections of society.[1]

[1] This was the case, too, in Germany about 1770.

The absence of an actual stage setting induced Seneca to include in his plays pieces of poetic description of nature, all (as was the case, too, with Vergil's descriptions) very appropriate to the situation. Such are, for example, the description by the chorus of the coming of dawn in *Hercules Furens*; the description of the simple life in the *Hippolytus*, where the " silent forest depths " suggest—in Racine's later play—Phèdre's passionate cry to be hidden with her lover in the shadow of the forests; the terror of the grove near Pelop's palace in *Thyestes*, where everything sways uncertainly—as in Vergil's description of the thunder-wind—and the star rushes across the sky " leaving a murky trail." The expression in the same play in which it is wished that the soil may lie heavy on the unholy head of Phædra is a primitive phrase, reminding us of the forcible expressions of both Greek and Elizabethan drama.

In certain ways the form of Seneca's tragedies illustrates their remoteness from the idea of a Greek tragedy. While the Greeks had a primitive moral law, including a sense of personal honour, the rights of the family, patriotic duty, and the necessity for a law of host and guest—all of which furnish the backbone of the drama[1]—the Greek tragedians allowed themselves to express frequently in the chorus a sympathy with Antigone who has committed a " sinless crime," and with Medea, treacherous and also betrayed, and with Œdipus in his unconscious sin, and with Hercules in his madness, and Phædra in her temptation, rightly relating the impulses and failures

[1] Cf. Euripides' *Alcestis*: Hercules was received as guest by Admetos and this brought about his recovery of Alcestis from the lower world ; Sophocles' *Antigone* contains the account of a conflict between filial duty and obedience to the State.

of the individual to their common human frailty and extolling the courage that surmounted it.

But Seneca, in a terror-driven and cruel age, could not let any sympathy appear with a character that had strained or broken a moral law. In that corrupt society the slightest failure would lead fatally to worse crime. Thus, while the chorus in the *Medea* of Euripides feels and expresses, through the Corinthian women, the inequality of relations between Jason and Medea, and her excuse for revenge, the chorus in Seneca's *Medea* merely laments the complexity of the times, and the unfortunate adventurousness of the Argonauts who brought Colchis into relation with Corinth. It looks forward sadly to the opening out of all lands. The sympathy is entirely for Jason as the sole survivor of the luckless and misdirected band of adventurers.

To this separation of interest shown by the chorus in Seneca the condition of the Roman stage contributed. For while the chorus in Greek drama could turn from actors to audience, inspire, condemn, or produce pity, the actors on the Roman stage were practically out of reach of the chorus. Their stage was more elevated but narrow and the action took place farther away from the spectator.

Sometimes, as in the *Hippolytus* of Seneca, the chorus describes in an entirely detached way the movements of the heavenly bodies, or the passion of love, or speaks cynically about Hippolytus' struggle with himself. Instead of adding new and illustrative rhythms to the march of events on the stage, as in Greek drama, the chorus of Seneca takes the place of the modern musical interlude between acts : where the relation between the music and the play is seldom that of mood or presage, but is of a quite commonplace order. We know how Scotch tunes and music-hall songs fill up intervals in a modern play, often without the slightest relation between the content of the tunes or songs and the emotional content of the acts they divide. Music in a modern play separates instead of combining the moments of a drama. Seneca's choruses produce an effect of a common greyness intervening between acts which show a play of highly-concentrated emotion. Seneca's choruses, however, have a delightful lyrical swing, though not much variety of treatment, as they are in the same metre in each play, and they contain the greater part of Seneca's nature pictures. From this point of view— to use another analogy—they resemble a rather pretty stage curtain which stays in its place for a long time, and which we get to know rather too well : and we wonder why that particular curtain is used. The Argive women in Seneca's *Agamemnon* so constantly commend moderation and the golden mean, that one wonders if they approve of tragedy as an art. They also utter flattering words about different Greek mythical heroes, and sometimes again the impression is produced of a complete *non sequitur*. The chorus was being driven out of its position in the theatre and in the play.

In one other direction Seneca's conception of tragedy included a rather commonplace view. In the *Agamemnon* of Æschylus, Cassandra, left alone upon the scene, falls into a frenzy, and describes the bloody deeds that will be done within the fatal palace she shudders to enter, and also her own end. She enlarges the meaning of the play by bringing the future into the present. In Seneca's version of the same play Cassandra is nearer the palace than to the chorus, and much farther from the spectators than in the Greek theatre. She is made to repeat aloud, just like a thought-reader, what is actually happening in the palace. There is therefore no idea of presage : she merely uses her power to translate a fact. The result is a great strain on the audience. Maeterlinck has made use of the same scheme in a play [1] in which the messenger of evil tidings looks in at the window of a house and describes the peaceful occupations of the unsuspecting victims of Fate. This, however, in Maeterlinck is the whole play, and it is his method of staging the inside of the house without bringing it visibly on the scene. As the messenger is using his natural senses, the eye and the ear, there is no strain to the audience, but in Seneca the situation is both overdone and commonplace. Seneca's Cassandra is like the blind beggar sitting on the steps in *Kismet*, really recognizing the passers-by, but not appearing to do so. In the modern melodrama, where characters are always rushing to the telephone and hearing sensational facts, we have the same effect as in Maeterlinck. There is nothing inartistic in this extension of the natural senses, which merely produces an unseen enlargement of the stage. It is, in fact, more in accordance with good tradition than is Seneca's theory.

It becomes evident that Seneca has not written plays that could be staged in any way convincing either to the ancient Roman or the modern mind. But standing as he does between Greek and mediæval drama, he suggests certain methods which are used by Shakespeare under different conditions.

From the tragedy of this present world Seneca appeals either to the Stoic quality in man himself, or to the knowledge of a larger justice, which is only reached through self-control, detachment and observance of the course of history. It is at moments when this world has nothing to offer but a contrast with

[1] *L'Intime.*

the ideal, and when disillusion is inevitable, that both Seneca and Shakespeare produce a sense of balance by calling in a new picture of something which is unattainable by present experience. This is a way in which the experience of life on the stage is extended. When Shakespeare calls in sleep— " that knits up the ravelled sleeve of care "—it is as a compensation to tragedy : when the harshest law is to take its course he calls upon the " quality of mercy." In the same way he allows Claudio to see a vision of courage and of purity, and Othello to see for a moment what is the faith he has not got, or Hamlet the gaiety he never will feel. Seneca, when Hercules is seized by mad fury, calls up sleep, in terms very similar to Shakespeare's. When Hercules is conceived of as a criminal and cumberer of the earth, Seneca calls out the elegiac quality of nature, mourning for her dead. When the furies are let loose in the play of *Thyestes*, the chorus calls upon all Greeks who love the twin harbours of Corinth and the " dissevered sea " to remember her, and her cool streams and lovely country. Œdipus in the *Phœnissæ*, when the Seven are against Thebes, talks of the beauty of peace.

All the characteristics above mentioned, but treated with a much freer hand, because the age of Nero had come to an end, occur in the one extant Roman historical drama, *Octavia*, probably written soon after Seneca's death. Here the chorus is simply attached to the interests of the family of Nero, and ceases to take the place of a chorus in the Greek sense. It has perhaps something of the function of the Elizabethan crowd, representing a point of view within the play. The nature word-pictures become more frequent and are placed in the mouths of the characters themselves : as, for instance, in that of Octavia. The structure of the play is historical and not legendary.

It is realistic, it makes the appeal of present politics to a people living in the assumed period of the play. It might be played on any stage and is quite independent of the historical accessories of the Greek and Roman drama.

CHAPTER II

MEDIÆVAL DRAMA

ONE of the subjects of Greek tragedy was destined to have a re-awakening in later dramatic art : this was the influence of supernatural forces on human life. We have seen that on the Greek stage devices were used for staging the gods of the upper air, and also the more earthly, local, and half-human deities. When they appeared, they affected the action of the play in a very noticeable manner. There was also in the later form of the Greek stage, and in certain forms of the Roman stage, derived from that of Greece, a device for housing spirits from the underworld, who appeared in the orchestra out of a kind of tunnel that came from below the stage.

Although the tradition for the production of a Greek play was lost in the Middle Ages, the actual plots and stories were well known to mediæval chroniclers, and the whole history of Troy was the field for adventures in lay drama when once serious classical plays were staged.[1] But in the early Middle Ages the subjects for drama were almost entirely dictated by the Chris-

[1] In the fourteenth and fifteenth centuries we have evidence of the imitation of the Classical Roman play in Italy. See W. Cloetta, *Beiträge zur Litteratur-Geschichte des Mittelatters und der Renaissance* (1890).

tian Church.[1] Christian records and Old Testament history were its main subjects. It was not, however, forgotten that there had once been a classical drama and a stage on which three forms of reality could be represented : an underworld, this present world, and a super-world, in only one of which would the action of a play take place. There might, however, be a prologue in another sphere : and figures from the upper or lower world might appear on the middle stage. The influence of this memory of a lost classical art on the stage form of the mediæval drama is one which appeared as soon as liturgical drama became " learned " drama.

This change affected much of the drama of the fourteenth and fifteenth centuries, and was especially noticeable in the sixteenth century.[2] But up to that date, i.e. from the tenth to the fifteenth centuries, the ecclesiastical influences of the age tended to stage religious drama in a way that recalled the church in which these plays were originally performed : thus such plays were acted at *stations* [3] rather than on *stages*.

[1] An exception, however, should be made in regard to the versions and imitations of Terence which were made in North Germany in the tenth century. These are a sign of an earlier renaissance of the classical spirit, and the most remarkable writer of the period was the nun Roswitha of Gandersheim, who wrote six versions of Terence, and composed six Latin prose comedies in imitation of the Latin author. In her original work there are religious elements drawn from her experience and profession, together with farcical elements, while a great vivacity of dialogue anticipates the more developed mediæval play.

[2] The origin of much of fourteenth- and fifteenth- century drama is not clearly established, but it is becoming evident that it owes less to folk-drama and more to authors who wrote with classical knowledge, or had written plays for the Universities, than has till recently been supposed.

[3] As in the Church the procession halted at each station of the Cross, so the sacred pageant or miracle play followed the same path.

Apart, however, from the actual form of the play, the supernatural elements which in a Greek play had helped to direct the action, found a very strong reflection in mediæval sacred drama, in which the art consisted in the concrete representation of supernatural forces. The prologue often represented a " war in heaven " which was afterwards shown to be worked out on earth. This was a new form of art. The Greek play had stressed the reality of the present conflict : the mediæval drama treated the reality of the earthly conflict as entirely dependent on certain spiritual conditions in another sphere.[1]

It will be convenient to trace the continental form of drama before comparing it with that of England. The first necessity of mediæval drama was to find some setting which should produce a unity of effect. In the Greek play the chorus had unified the scenes. by looking backward to history and forward to new events. When sacred subjects were staged for the education and pleasure of the people, the only two types of setting available were the Gospel narrative in its simplest form, and (more frequently) the liturgy of the Church, with its psalms and anthems, introits and antiphons, its versicles and responses, its lessons and exhortations : its great acts in the presence of God : its processions winding round church, cloister, and churchyard, and through the towns from one sacred place to another. On Good Friday, throughout

---

[1] Probably the eclipse of Seneca from the tenth to the thirteenth centuries, and of the tradition for which he stood, was favourable to the new art of sacred drama. When at the Renaissance classical models recovered their position, they gave a new form to a mediæval tradition which was by that time well established. In the neo-classical drama, from the seventeenth century onwards, we can see how the classical and mediæval traditions combined to found a third type of art.

Christendom, the procession in the churches stopped
at each station of the Cross. Litanies were sung in
the fields in the ploughing season, replacing the pagan
fertility rites. The Easter service included a dialogue
between the Marys and the Angel at the Sepulchre,
which then, as now in Catholic countries, was staged
at the east end of the church, or " under the altar,"
as was the scene of Christmas in a stable at the west
end. The appeal of the Christian rite was human, and
because it was human it was also dramatic, and taught
its lessons through reference to concrete experience.

Sometimes scenes represented in the churches were
based on the pseudo-Augustine's list of the prophet
witnesses to Christ,[1] or on the chapter " By Faith "
in the Epistle to the Hebrews (Heb. xi.). At Furnes,
in Belgium, the stations of the Cross were marked
in the streets outside the church, and the officials of
the town had their parts assigned in the Good Friday
procession. Usually, however, priests and choristers
took the parts. Angels, heaven-sent shepherds, and
prophets appeared from a door in the east end of
the church : demons from another part towards the
west.[2] By the end of the eleventh century the drama-
tizing of incidents in the Gospels and in the lives
of the Prophets was general, but the first definite
play is found in the middle of the twelfth century,
and is called the *Sponsus*, a dramatic form of the
parable of the wise and foolish virgins. This is of
French origin, and consists of a Latin chorus, followed
by dialogue in Latin and French. When the foolish

[1] See Mâle, *L'Art Religieux du XIIe siècle en France.*
[2] The rubrics or directions for acting the drama show the
simplicity of the representation. In the play *The Conversion
of St. Paul* the cities of Damascus and Jerusalem are suggested
by seats on which the actors stood. In the Norman-French
Adam, characters in Paradise only showed head and shoulders
above curtains which screened their movements.

virgins are spurned by the Bridegroom, and cursed in French, they are seized by demons and thrown into hell (presumably the crypt of the church). The ambulatory of a church supplied a convenient place whence the *vox ex alto* could be heard, as for example in the later play, *The Conversion of St. Paul*, acted at Fleury-sur-Loire.

The attempt at dramatic form then produced a double movement : the first is connected with a conception of the three planes of reality and the other with the idea of the different stations at which separate scenes could be acted.[1] The next stage was the presentation of the play outside the church : as with the longer play of *Adam*, and here we have very careful stage directions. The Creator appears from the church itself, tells Adam and Eve how to act in Paradise : he then goes back into the church. Demons appear, running hither and thither in the square, and tempt Adam, who resists : then they confer again, and finally tempt Eve, who succumbs. The Creator and the angel with the drawn sword appear from the church at intervals. The demons constantly plant thorns in the path of Adam and Eve and finally carry both persons off to hell.

When it became a custom to represent successive scenes of this character outside the church, something of the pageant form was evolved, and wagons containing *tableaux vivants* of the scenes passed through the crowded streets. These took the place of a single

[1] This fact can be illustrated from later groups of liturgical plays : as for example from the three plays of Hilarius, pupil of Abelard. The third of these, an episode in the story of a statue of St. Nicholas, *Le Jeu de l'image de St. Nicholas*, needs a movement on the ground floor (robbers steal a barbarian's treasure at the foot of the statue) and also the appearance of the Saint in a higher plane to confute the barbarian and confound the robbers.

group forming itself anew at every station.[1] The
street or the square then became the neutral ground
across which the action passed.

With the performance of stationary plays (not having
the pageant form) outside the church, a prologue
defining the cause of the play became usual. Thus
a Nativity play was prefaced by a prologue about
the Fall.

An outdoor stage, usually about five feet high,
with steps and ladders, and upper and lower floors
to the wooden sheds at the back of the stage, was
added to enable more people to see the drama,[2] and
the play was often made inordinately long, to include
lively scenes of ordinary life, as in Bodel's *Jeu de St.
Nicholas*. In Rutebœuf's *Le Miracle de Théophile*
(thirteenth century) we see a new element, for the
play centres in the possession of the soul of Théophile
(here we have the germ of the Faust *motif*), and while
we see the struggle depicted in his own mind, we
also see the Virgin on the one hand and the evil angel
on the other, externalizing and illustrating the mental
struggle. In a play like this, it was more convincing
to the audience to see the Virgin on one side rather than
above, the devil on the other, rather than below.[3]

---

[1] There is here a possible reflection of the flat platform
in a Greek play which presented the tableaux of an act which
had secretly taken place at the back of the stage.

See Karl Mantzius, *History of Theatrical Art*, Vol. II, in
which he collects the evidence in France, Germany, and
Switzerland for the development of the setting from the
open space backed by the church wall to a low stage with
booths or sheds in the space of the walls, and finally to the
Valenciennes stage with the " mansions " for each scene.
The stage grows in size with the popularity of the " mystère "
and the increasing length of the story acted.

[3] There was a definite influence on late thirteenth-century
religious plays on the Continent which is traceable to the
Meditations of Bonaventura (died 1274). In the illustrations

French plays then began to assume the form known as that of the " Mansions," with hell at one end of the stage and heaven on the other. This always seemed to occur when the issue of the conflict was doubtful, while if it was a foregone conclusion, the heaven above and the hell beneath were the proper conditions of the narrative play.

In the long series of the *Miracles de Notre Dame* (1340), narrative and incident are provided, and historical and legendary themes are freely treated. In all these plays the intervention of Our Lady provides a solution of the crisis in human life. In staging such plays, therefore, it was necessary to have an elevated platform for the appearance of Our Lady, and one sufficiently extended for the presentation of incident. Stairs or short ladders led from the lower stage to the higher level.

From the twelfth to the fifteenth centuries there is, however, very little record of any fixed plan for the production of mystery plays or other ecclesiastical plays. For, from the time when these plays were acted outside the churches, the stages were movable and arranged according to convenience on each occasion. So long as the church supplied the background for the stage, the evidence of the " rubrics " goes to prove that the actors came on from the church and went off to the church. But while this applies to the play of *Adam*, the earliest for which we possess any directions, we hear later that when the stage became detached from the church, booths with curtains, representing hell and paradise, and other *loci* served to lodge the characters not in action on the stage, and to conceal them when they changed their dresses.

to this book we have a very fresh and concrete setting of the sacred story : and familiar details are added from contemporary Italian life.

This appears as early as the twelfth century in the
fragment of a Resurrection mystery. We have also
allusions to characters seated on the stage, and considered therefore to be " off " unless actually standing
or reciting : and in the fifteenth century mention is
made of a curtained alcove which served for the representation of events off the stage of which an account was
given. The most complete representation of a fifteenth-
century stage occurs in the title page by Jean Fouquet to
the mystery of the martyrdom of St. Apollonia,[1] while
the stage of the sixteenth century is illustrated by
the record of the Valenciennes Passion Play in 1547.

The audience at first appeared to stand before the
stage ; but mention is made in 1437, in the Metz town
chronicle, of seats arranged at different levels for the
accommodation of nobles and ladies.[2]

A very complete set of stage directions for the
Mystère represented at Mons in 1501 has been recently
recovered, and bears out our knowledge of the elaborate character of the " machines " used at that period.
Amiens and Chauny lent their properties, and Amiens
lent the tent. The stage was more than 40 yards
long and about 20 wide, and stood against a row of
houses in the Grand'-Place. The stage itself was
covered with earth and grass, to suit the illusion
of the " mansions " appearing on a field. A " parcque"
was seated for spectators. At the back of the stage
were the various " mansions " or edifices, painted in
bright heraldic colours. Canopies with sun and
moon and golden stars hung over paradise ; a tent
protected hell " plein de bruit, de flammes, de grimaces
et de menaces." Serpents made of basket-work
crawled on the stage near Lucifer, and a " machine "

[1] See G. Bapst, *Essai sur l'histoire du Théâtre*, p. 33.
[2] See Les Frères Parfaict, *Histoire du Théâtre Français*,
pp. 49–53.

for making thunder enhanced the terror of the place. Towers and castles, representing Rome, Bethlehem and Nazareth, flanked the stage between hell and paradise : where God the Father, clad in a fur-trimmed robe and wearing gloves, sat surrounded by angels. The " mystère " thus presented covered the history of the world, from the Creation to the Resurrection of our Lord.[1]

The fifteenth century marks a separation between the play which closely follows the sacred text and the more lay variant of it. It was then that the word " mystère " implied dramatic action and not only tableaux. It also marks the attempted fusion of older plays into a long Old Testament cycle and a New Testament one. These contain judgment scenes in which God, Justice, and Mercy appear.[2] The pleading for and against the soul attains immense importance in French drama : and at times the law court, rather than the church, becomes the model of the stage[3] : in Greban's *Mystère de la Passion* the whole of the powers of heaven and hell are seen striving for the souls of the human race.[4] In none of these plays is there any element that corresponds to Fate, or to an unexpected happening which precipitates action. God is the Judge of the world, and the

[1] By M. Gustave Cohen, Professor at the University of Strassburg. See Mélanges offerts à M. G. Lanson, 1922.

[2] The little play *La Passion de Notre Frère le Poilu*, written during the war of 1914–18, is on the model of a fifteenth-century "mystère."

[3] This occurs too in the *Miracles de Notre Dame*, where a legal point is often seized upon to give a reason for the interference of Heaven with the affairs of earth. The logic of the Schoolmen is reproduced in the play, together with the language of the law courts.

[4] These were confraternity plays, and in contrast with Greek drama have many characters. Greban's has 244 speaking parts besides the supers.

strings of Fate are in His hand. A religious atmosphere common to actors and audience gives the necessary unity to the play. The only time when tragic doubt assumes any real force is (1) when Judas is uncertain about his action and (2) when the devils return to hell and wait to see if Christ will really succeed in breaking down the gates.

When a rationalizing tendency came about in the fifteenth century, the problem of human life was decided in a disconcertingly rapid way, and super-natural events became hardly distinguishable from ordinary human incidents. Spiritual reality had been made common in the effort to define it. In Italy we have the account of a mystery in pageant form at Florence in 1340,[1] which, though performed at the May Kalends, thus recalling a pagan festival, had scenes from the Old and New Testaments and a scene of judgment. It appears too that confraternity plays were known at the same period, and probably earlier.[2] These representations had been given at Rome within the precincts of the Coliseum, but were forbidden in that place by Pope Paul III in 1549, when the French confraternity plays were also forbidden at the Hôtel de Bourgogne.

While religious drama had its origin in the sacred tableaux displayed coincidently with the Church service, or just before it, on the holy days of the Church, lay drama had its origin in the acts of the revellers who went from house to house, sometimes in disguise, and played there or in the streets and squares of a town. Groups of bourgeois or artisans formed a

[1] On the evidence of Vasari.

[2] See Riccoboni, *Reflexions sur les Théâtres*. He assumes that the confraternity " del gonfalone," founded in 1264, existed primarily for the performance of mystery plays. The Statutes of the Confraternity (1584) give colour to this view.

confederacy, lightly held together and easily dissolved, for the presentation of rough farces.[1] Two of these groups became important in Paris, the " basochiens," or corporations of actors drawn from groups of lawyers and lawyers' clerks, and the " Enfants sans souci," who reproduced in the city the merrymaking and pageantry and the blunt satire of the Feast of Fools, which had been a parody on the Church, its services and its organization, and had been driven out from the feasts of the Church's year. Their plays were known as " soties."[2]

About the year 1470 appeared a play, *Maître Pathelin*, with considerably more form and promise than earlier dramatic attempts. The actors of this play and others on the same lines were accustomed to march on to a rough stage (or into a hall) in procession, carrying the properties necessary for the presentation of their piece. Having arranged them, the piece was acted, and then the actors, in a line, saluted the audience and went away as they had come.[3] The French habit of the distinction of " genres " kept this type of comedy apart from the " sotie," and a programme was frequently made up of a " mystère," a " sotie," and a farce, the same actors appearing in each. An art intermediate between that of the mystery play and the " sotie " was that of the morality, played by actors who emphasized the romantic and pathetic

[1] In *A Midsummer Night's Dream* Shakespeare reminds us of the survival of this custom in England in his day.

[2] In collections of " soties " " la mère sote " is represented between two actors in the livery of the " Enfants." As late as 1863 the guild of carpenters in Paris went to Mass in procession, headed by their " mère." See V. Fournel, *Les Spectacles populaires*, pp. 6, 7.

[3] The appearance of the actors for the bidding prayer at the end of an Elizabethan play was a survival of a similar early custom.

character of a piece to which a moral was attached.
The staging of a morality was more elaborate than
that of a farce. As there was less action, more emphasis was laid on the type or character represented on
the stage ; and dress and surroundings became important in defining that type. An interesting parallel
can be found in the pageantry by which Paris and
other cities welcomed a new king or a king's bride,
and which generally took the form of allegorical
figures staged on a platform at the city gates.[1] Between
the reigns of Charles V and Francis I this custom
prevailed : but in the reign of Francis I the allegorical
tableau gave way to the classical triumphal arch.
Considerable light is thrown on the structure of the
morality by the study of the tableaux, which contained the figures which were shown in action in a
morality play, and like the morality had a chorus of
musicians and many allegorical devices attached to
it. A study of these types of art also shows that
the moving spirit in the tableau or " représentation "
was that of the city ; and that the work was done by
the cultivated bourgeoisie of the time. It had a
civic and not an ecclesiastic origin : it was not derived
from court influences nor carried out by university
actors. The advent of the king or queen before
the platform was the signal for a movement in the
tableau and for music from the choir. In most cases
a " Lit de Justice " was represented : and the conflict
between Nature and Grace, a subject of thought in
the cultivated society of the time, was pictorially
presented. The morality play attached the symbolic

[1] See Les Frères Parfaict, *Histoire du Théâtre Français*,
Vol. II, p. 148 *et seq.*, for the entry of Isabeau of Bavaria in
1389, Henry VI in 1431, Charles VII 1437, Louis XI 1461,
Louis XII 1498, Anne of Brittany 1504, Mary of England
1514, Claude 1517, Eleanor of Austria 1530.

idea to a concrete narrative, and is found to follow the " représentation " at an interval of more than a century. In 1389 we have the first account of a " représentation," in 1511 of a " moralité."

We now come to a critical period for France—the middle of the sixteenth century. It was in 1548 that the " Confrères de la Passion " were forbidden in future to act sacred plays. These were considered by some to be mediæval and crude, by others to be too daring, and possibly also superstitious. It is a matter of literary history that the hall used by the Confrères [1] was given up to the performance of other plays. Jodelle, Garnier, Monchrétien, Hardy wrote plays of the Classical Revival, using the old Greek *motifs* staged by the methods of the Latin play. Corneille's *Cid*, with its frequent changes of scene, was produced on the stage of the " many mansions " in 1636.

The development of mediæval sacred drama in England in its early stages is necessarily close to the evolution in France, with which country from the tenth to the twelfth centuries England was so nearly connected. In the fourteenth century, however, cycles of sacred drama were written in English and assumed an immense proportion, lasting from the story of the Creation to the Last Judgment. [2]

The English version of the mystery play tended to abandon the fixed stage and the fixed form. The actors toured about the town and performed a pageant, with episodes staged on wagons. This was the case

[1] Salle du Petit Bourbon. This hall had a stage about forty-eight feet wide, which was reached from the pit by a flight of steps. Above the stage was a loggia with a balcony (from a description dated 1613).

[2] A modern cinema play called the " Photo-Drama of Creation " covers the same ground in pictures.

with the York and Chester plays : and the fact tended
to the simplification of incident and to a strong presentation of certain scenes. The legal arguments and
the conflict over the soul are both left out of what
becomes the effective staging of a well-known story.
There were very few plays of the life-history of a saint ;
these always ended in a martyrdom and were common
in France, where they formed, in fact, the pattern
for Corneille's *Polyeucte*. In England the scheme is
always so large as to be apocalyptic. And certainly,
in the description of the fall of Lucifer in the Coventry
cycle, the scenes in the unseen world contain the
quality of tragic surprise that had not been called
in to enhance the interest of the French play. For
the scenes in heaven, as defined in the play, are well
conceived and forcible, and suggest the kind of character-study afterwards developed by Milton. It is
earth, with her weakness and wickedness, that gives
the shock to the life of heaven, and gives its strength
to hell. Earth produces this dislocation in the spiritual world by her misuse of free-will. Cain scoffs at
God. Man, too, is represented according to Scrip-
ture in the scene of temptation in the Garden of
Eden. He hears God's voice, but does not see Him
in person. Such a theory gives force to the representation of both worlds, since it is in accordance
with human experience. Occasionally, however, God
speaks, and also appears in a prologue. Where this
is the case, this part of the processional pageant comes
independently on to the scene. In the *Transfigura-
tion* of the York play, heaven, earth, and hell are all
forcibly expressed. Sometimes, as in the Chester
Judgement, types, such as pope, emperor, king, and
queen appear instead of individuals, and dramatic
action is lost in the recitation scheme.[1] But the

[1] This use of types reappears in Marlowe's *Dr. Faustus*.

personification of types prepares us for one form, the English sacred drama, in which the seen and unseen worlds are connected. As in the *Danse Macabre* on the Continent, death comes in as a familiar and intimate figure in all the details of ordinary human life.[1]

We see in English plays the externalization of soul and body. An instance of this is the *Lazarus* play, where the corruption of the body is imaginatively described. In a still earlier play, the soul externalized upbraids the body for its corruption. " Thou hast no friend who would not flee, if thou camest stumbling in the street." All this has a reflection later on in the Elizabethan drama.

The English morality, representing the conflict between good and evil, dealt either with the allegorical presentment of the human race, as in the *Castle of Perseverance*, or with the life-history of an individual, typifying the human race, as in *Everyman*. In both cases the stage setting became symbolic to fit in with the allegory expressed by the characters. " Everyman " lives out the span of human life, and traverses the space of his wanderings, on the few boards of the mediæval stage. His progress was marked therefore by steps and by symbolic objects on the path : considerable emphasis was laid on word and gesture, which were slow and distinct, if monotonous, and on costume, which was striking and appropriate. Demons and angels and effects of light and darkness still further enhanced the sensation of the play.

[1] See the Coventry *Slaughter of the Innocents*. For further illustration, see E. K. Chambers, *The Mediæval Stage*, and Whitmore, *The Supernatural in Tragedy*. From time to time mysteries were forbidden on account of the irreverent interludes in them. In 1384 William of Wykeham turned them out of the cathedral and graveyard at Winchester. In 1574 they were finally forbidden.

A somewhat similar effect was obtained by the dumb-show, organized by trade guilds all over Europe on Corpus Christi Day. The show itself tended to disappear from the sixteenth century onwards, leaving only the procession.[1] But certain variants of it appear in the allegorical pageant which was in use in England, as in France, to celebrate the entry of kings and visitors of state into her cities. Existing records are later in England than in France, but the influence of the crafts or guilds on the structure of the tableaux, and the accompaniment of a choir, point to a similar origin. The most elaborate tableaux or pageants, as they were called (even when there was no moving out of fixed positions), were produced after the victories of the Hundred Years War.[2] When Henry V returned from Agincourt in 1415 he was met at London Bridge by allegorical tableaux and by music. Henry VI, after his entry into Paris in 1431, was welcomed in London by magnificent tableaux, in which were figures of Nature, Grace, Fortune, the Sciences and the Virtues. In 1522, on a later occasion, London provided eleven pageants to welcome Charles V of Germany. All the Tudor kings and queens were received with pageants at their royal entries. Pageants and moralities dealt with similar subjects and both reflected the topics of civic life.[3]

[1] The modern survival is the Lord Mayor's Show.

[2] The first pageant of this kind was invented to celebrate the marriage of Henry III with Eleanor of Provence. As many of the earliest civic pageants in France originated in Provence, this fact has its interest.

[3] Gigantic figures, such as those of Gog and Magog in the town of Winchester, the dragon at Norwich, and Hob-Nob at Salisbury, form a part of civic processions in Belgium and in Provence as well as in England, and appear to denote the forces of evil which have been overcome. In 1922 similar grotesque figures were noted in town fairs and commemorations in Alsace.

At the same period a new art was introduced into English life, that of the *Interlude*, which has a closer link with the coming Elizabethan drama than pageants or moralities possessed. Interludes were short pieces, of a farcical nature, intended to be performed in the pauses of a banquet or other entertainment. The actors of these short plays were itinerant, but they acted within doors, in the halls of great houses and of the trade guilds. They also used the courtyards of inns, thus anticipating the Elizabethan players. The company was usually a small one, and put itself under the protection of some noble, whose livery was worn by these players. The practice, common in England in the Court from about 1464, when these players were acknowledged to be excepted from sumptuary laws, was also common at the French Court and in great houses on the Continent. Even now the Comédie Française dresses some of its minor characters in plays of the seventeenth and eighteenth centuries in the royal livery of the appropriate date.

Interludes had already been acted towards the end of the fifteenth century at Oxford and Cambridge, where the college halls were visited by the players from great houses. But the custom in the universities was to allow the students to entertain their own and other colleges at Twelfth Night, or at Shrovetide or Mid-Lent Carnival, times given up to the sway of the Lord of Misrule, who with his troupe parodied the government of the university and the Church. The survival of these customs can probably be traced in the disturbances at Commemoration which lasted up to the period of the War of 1914–18.

When interludes were played indoors, and in rooms where the rich colour of panelled walls and carved galleries supplied a suitable background, staging became an ingenious adaptation of the play to the particular conditions of the moment. As the interlude was frankly farcical it depended very little on stage properties or scenery. But from 1564 onwards there are records of elaborate plans both for fixed and movable scenery, and for stage formation in the Vitruvian manner, whenever plays were commanded by royalty, or given at universities or in halls, frequently in honour of some member of the royal house. The influences which brought about this development were Italian, and were connected with the close contact of England with the Italy of the New Learning.

CHAPTER III

THE DRAMA OF THE RENAISSANCE

TOWARDS the end of the fifteenth century the revival of Roman plays in Italy was encouraged by the classical academies of the period (in Rome from about 1484 and in Ferrara from 1471), and was only interrupted in 1527 by the fall of Rome. Coincidently with representations of Plautus and imitations of his manner on restored Roman stages throughout Italy came the publication in 1486 of Vitruvius' *De Architectura*, which had been known in manuscript since 1414, and which described the early Roman theatres. While one effect of the knowledge of the construction of these theatres was seen in the building at Ferrara of a permanent theatre for Ariosto's plays (which was destroyed in 1533) and of the great theatre at Vicenza at a later date, the more general influence of Vitruvius may be noticed in the interest taken in Italy in the staging of plays, with scenery both in the form of mural painting, of sculptured backgrounds, and of movable painted and decorative perspective scenes,[1] and also with scenes which are removed to disclose other scenes beyond. It has been suggested by recent writers [2] that the paraphernalia in use on the stage of the sixteenth

[1] See L. B. Campbell, *Scenes and Machines on the English Stage during the Renaissance.* 1923. Ch. 1.
[2] See the work of Miss Campbell, op. cit.

43

century in England was clearly derived from the Italian stage of the fifteenth century, where the apparatus was used on classical authority.

Another important development in stage-setting can be directly referred to Italy of the fifteenth century— that is, the application of the laws of perspective to stage scenery. The most important steps in this direction were taken when Leonardo da Vinci had urged a geometrical basis for painting and sculpture, and when Albert Dürer had invented instruments for perspective drawing. Barbaro published in 1559 a work on perspective, in which he discussed its application to stage scenery. Similar works appeared in France.[1] In 1545 Serlio collected all hitherto available knowledge on the subject, and made it clear (1) that the front part of the stage should be on a level with the eye of the onlooker, (2) that the back part should be inclined, and should be higher by one-ninth than the front part. The sixteenth-century Italian stage with its houses, or solid " sets " to right and left, its drop-scene behind the central open space, was transmitted to France by the Italian actors, and, as there constructed, was a natural simplification of the classical method. It was clearly in the minds of Serlio and those who worked on his plan that the empty space must be filled with incident, and that dummies should move across it while the real characters were absent. This perhaps is a memory of the silent actors on the Greek and Roman classical stage : but it is the first account of the representation of a play with the help of paste-board figures which developed later into the Italian marionette show.

Italy built her theatres in the sixteenth century [2]

[1] J. Cousin, Livre de la Perspective. 1560.

[2] See Vitruvius, De Architectura, Book V, ch. 3, on the construction of theatres, which was followed by Italian architects from the fifteenth century onwards.

on the model that is familiar to us at Orange, and carried on the Roman tradition in tragedy. The " Teatro Olimpico " at Vicenza still exists, and possesses a full architectural scena. There are the three classic doors on the stage, two exits from the proscenium, rows of statues and columns ; the whole painted very unconvincingly, since for scenic purposes the alleys were made to diverge instead of converging in perspective. The fierce emotion of Italian tragedy, not unlike that of Seneca's Roman plays, rushes at once from impression to action, and needs a steady, solid architectural background.[1]

In France and England much rougher and simpler construction was being used. This was partly due to the fact that the full effect of the neo-classical stage was not felt in England till the works of Vitruvius and Serlio were translated into English ;[2] but another influence was at work in England, France, and Spain which was destined to produce a new art of the stage.

Both in France and England this new art of the sixteenth century was developed by bands of strolling players,[3] who played in booths at fairs, or—in England —in the inn yards, on a rough platform. These conditions controlled the future development of the form of the theatre. The actors used historical and legendary plots, but staged them in a way which closely represented the life of the author's period.

In 1576 the first theatre was built in London by

[1] The plays of Alfieri, written at Pisa on the classic model in the years of the French Revolution, produce a remarkable contrast with an architectural background on the Italian stage.

[2] The translation of Serlio's work was published in 1611 : an abridgment of the De Architectura of Vitruvius in 1692. In France, Vitruvius was translated as early as 1547.

[3] The interlude, already discussed, was an early form of the new comedy.

John Barbage, in Holywell Lane, Shoreditch.[1] In 1599 the Globe was built; it was, however, burnt down in 1613. Others known at the same period are the Rose and the Swan, and the Fortune—theatres in Whitcross Street and Golding Lane; these are marked on a map of London dated 1616.

The shape of these buildings was octagonal or square : and the walls were filled with boxes which recalled the gallery of the inn yard and its balconies. There was a central platform, overhung by the balcony of the actors' house, which had an exit on each side. A curtain hung over the balcony, which was drawn if the balcony was used for a scene, and another curtain hung below screening the place beneath the balcony, which was used if necessary and enclosed a third door. Thus it became Juliet's tomb, while the balcony could be her balcony or the walls of Rome. The curtains—red for a sacred drama—were " perse " or blue-black for a tragedy, and other colours were used for comedies.[2] Where light was used at the end of a dark afternoon it was given by lamps at the

[1] In the same year a small private theatre was opened at Blackfriars, and marks a development which was different from that of the public theatre, for artificial light was used and the appeal was to a cultivated audience.

In this it resembled the theatre in France in a later period. As the acting was non-professional, it became a field for the child-player, and Shakespeare alluded to the fact that the children of the Chapel Royal and of St. Paul's were engaged in the art.

" But there is, sir, an eyry of children, little eyases, that cry out on the top of question, and are most tyrannically clapped for it, these are now the fashion."—*Hamlet*, Act II, sc. 2. Unlike the public plays, these private plays had musical intervals provided by the choir boys, and the plays were thus divided into acts. In this, too, the English private theatre resembled the French. (See W. J. Lawrence, *Times iterary Supplement*, August 11, 1921.)

[2] The custom of changing the colour of the curtains seems to have been by no means invariable.

side of the stage. The theatre was open to the air;
the actors lived in the actors' house : the plays were
performed from two o'clock in the afternoon : and
it became the habit for the gallants to have seats on
the front part of the stage. A very realistic play had
a stage-crowd to mingle with them and comment
on the play. This would have occurred during the
acting of the play-scene in *Hamlet*, and throughout
the performance of the *Knight of the Burning Pestle*.[1]

Our knowledge of these theatres is derived partly
from a sketch copied from one of the Swan Theatre,
made by Johannes de Witt, and preserved in the
University Library at Utrecht : and partly from a
reconstruction made by Godfrey in 1907 of the Fortune
Theatre from builders' specifications.

The size of the theatre was about 80 × 43 feet,
the common dimensions of its model the inn yard.

The part of the platform, the proscenium, which
projected into the centre, or pit, was about 18 feet
deep. The pit was in some cases used for bear-baiting,
when not filled with spectators at a play.

It will be observed that properties rather than
scenery were characteristic of the Elizabethan stage.
A trap-door for the emergence of a ghost was made
in the proscenium, where it served alike for the ghost
in *Hamlet* and for the grave-digging in the same play.
For staging Marlowe's *Faust* or sacred drama a movable
hell's mouth was also provided.[2]

We are accustomed to hear of the rapid and clear

[1] The *Beggars' Opera*, 1728, had two characters, including
the author, present as spectators. This is a late example of
the old custom.

[2] In 1584 Higgins's *Nomenclator* contained the substance
of Pollux's account of the " machines " of the Greek stage,
which can be seen to correspond in great part with those
used in Renaissance theatres. See L. B. Campbell, *Scenes
and Machines on the English Stage*.

speech of Elizabethan actors. They came in naturally, speaking their parts as they moved from the back to the front of the stage : it would have been impossible to imagine their coming on silently, taking up a position, and then delivering a speech, as could be done on the narrow French stage. Their position, on the apron or proscenium, right in the midst of the theatre, made it possible to them to speak easily and rapidly and still to be heard clearly. In the modern stage the apron has been cut back, and room made for the orchestra. The stage then appears as in a frame made by the section of the theatre, and the same effect of remoteness is obtained as on the French stage. But this is not according to Elizabethan tradition.[1]

It is due to a stage feeling which in England tends to make all presentations of the supernatural real and vivid, together with a method of constructing the stage which lends itself to that idea, that Elizabethan serious drama transformed the plots and characterization of Seneca's plays while at the same time making full use of them.

It has been said [2] that the supernatural figures in Seneca's plays were merely decorative in effect. They were, in fact, as much a part of the scenery as the columns and statues by which they stood. In the English versions of these plays, from 1560 onwards, the deities and the spirits become forcible characters. The versions deliberately add to the original with this view. So in Heywood's version of the *Troades*, Achilles' ghost, only referred to in the original, comes on the stage and has speeches assigned to it.[3]

[1] See *Quarterly Review*, April, 1908, article " Elizabethan Stage," and R. Crompton Rhodes, *The Stagery of Shakespeare*.
[2] Whitmore, *Supernatural in Tragedy*.
[3] See E. M. Spearing's *Elizabethan Translations of Seneca's Tragedies*, and Studley's *Translations of Seneca's Agamemnon and Medea*.

The Latin dramas, composed in the Elizabethan age, show the same tendency : and spirits from above and below the earth definitely affect the action of the play. In English plays, such as *Gorboduc*, 1562, it is expressly stated that the furies " came from under the stage as though out of hell." [1]

It is clear that on the English stage, nothing that affects the future life or the moral nature of man is left to the imagination of the audience. The author has, in every case, so strongly visualized the unseen world, that he brings it on to the plane of human drama. In Kyd's *Spanish Tragedy*, where the supernatural beings remain presumably outside the action " to serve as chorus in this tragedie," their hand is felt all the way through in the happenings on the stage. It becomes fairly evident that in the presentation of *Macbeth*, Shakespeare brought a very concrete ghost of Banquo upon the scene. The ghost was such a striking reality, in fact, that the oddity lay in not seeing it. This is definitely Elizabethan in spirit. Marlowe's *Dr. Faustus*, very full of supernatural events, was realistically presented. Witches and incantations, to bring about the connexion between the present world and the world unseen, are very characteristic of Elizabethan drama. [2]

To the mind of a modern playgoer there might be something lacking in an Elizabethan stage production : but this lack was supplied in the dialogue and —a more important point—by the dramatic appeal of the play. As there was no scenery (strictly speaking),

---

[1] Aristotle's *Poetics* had familiarized writers of the Renaissance with the idea that " spectacle " could produce a secondary effect of terror. *Poetics*, XIV. 1, 2.

[2] In Peele's *Edward I*, Marston's *Sophonisba*, Shakespeare's *Julius Cæsar*, Heywood's *Late Lancashire Witches*, the action is dominated in turn by the living man and the spirits.

4

the attention of the audience was concentrated on the action, and the colour and atmosphere that we connect with scenery and lighting were produced by the poetical images in the words of the actors. The curtain or awning over the actors' house was of blue material, spangled with stars and reinforced by the sun and moon.[1] At any time in the action an actor would point to the symbolized sunlight, moonlight, or star-light, while darkness was represented by the bringing of artificial light on to the stage [2] : torches were carried when the scene was supposed to be out of doors, candles for an indoor scene.

POR. " How far that little candle throws his beams,
      So shines a good deed in a naughty world.
NER. When the moon shone we did not see the candle." [3]

That the dramatic appeal of a great play is inde-pendent of the scenery and staging is sufficiently proved by the vitality of the plays of Shakespeare and his greater contemporaries. We have, however, an explicit statement from Ben Jonson, in the prologue to *Every Man in His Humour*, that the play he pre-sents is independent of stage devices,[4] and in the

---

[1] Cf. Holinshed's account of the preparation for a play in 1520 (Vol. III, p. 635): ". . . and the roofe was covered with blue sattin set full of presses of fine gold. . . ."

[2] As in the fifteenth-century nativity plays where Joseph carries a lighted lantern to contrast with the imagined darkness.

[3] Act V, sc. 1. The *Merchant of Venice* is full of references to natural and artificial light. See Act V, sc. 1:
    This night, methinks, is but the daylight sick;
    It looks a little paler, 'tis a day
    Such as the day is when the sun is hid.
And :
    How sweet the moonlight sleeps upon the bank!

[4] Where neither chorus wafts you o'er the seas ;
    Nor creaking throne comes down, the boyes to please,
    Nor nimble squibbe is seene, to make afear'd

introduction to *Every Man out of His Humour* he expresses himself as opposed to constant changes of scene. Shakespeare, too, in the prologue to *Henry V* calls up the audience to

" Piece out our imperfections with your thoughts,"

more especially as the theme he has chosen is one which can only be symbolically represented on the stage.

> " Can this Cock-Pit hold
> The vasty fields of France, or may we cram
> Within this wooden O the very casques
> That did affright the air at Agincourt ? "

Shakespeare held that the prologue, with its appeal to the imagination of the audience, took the place of the Roman chorus :

> " Admit me Chorus to this History."

Historical dress on the stage was a thing unknown to the Elizabethans ; but the atmosphere of history was produced in a Roman play by throwing a toga over the court dress. Dress played a certain part in the plot. For example, instances of confused identity, as in the *Comedy of Errors*, make the play almost unintelligible when staged according to modern ideas. But when, as probably was the case on the Elizabethan stage, the twin brothers and the two Dromios were different in personal appearance, while the pairs of twins were dressed alike, the audience could enter into the fun by recognizing an identity or a change of character that was understood to be veiled to the actors. The inherent improbability of

> The gentlewomen ; nor roul'd bullet heard
> To say, it thunders, nor tempestuous drumme
> Rumbles, to tell you when the storme doth come.

See on this subject, L. B. Campbell, *Scenes and Machines on the English Stage*.

the ship splitting in two at the time of the wreck, leaving one brother and one servant in each half, presented no difficulty to an Elizabethan audience. It was a given condition of the play. But actors, not only dressed alike, but made up to be physically alike, would have confused such an audience.

The form of the play was also affected by the shape and conditions of the theatre. In most of Shakespeare's plays we have two groups of actors, representing an inner plot and a sub-plot—as in the *Merchant of Venice*, or *A Midsummer Night's Dream*, with the court as a general setting for the play. As is well known, the actors issued on the stage from the right and left of the actors' house, and there were no curtains to mark the ends of acts or scenes. Acts were a later division imposed on Shakespeare's plays. There was one pause after the crisis. In the *Merchant of Venice* this occurs after the Trial Scene.

Divisions into scenes were implied by the exits and entrances, for which directions were given in the Quartos. Other directions for the conduct of a scene became necessary when in *Henry IV* or *Richard III* or the three parts of *King Henry VI* a conflict between armies was represented by the fringe of the fight with people flying and pursuing, and by occasional single combats. It is characteristic of Shakespeare to give the impression of a battle from " another part of the field " and to repeat this method, without attempting to bring the real mêlée on to the stage. It was evidently understood that opposing elements (such as rival armies) entered from the doors to right and left of the stage, and that the door under the balcony frequently referred to a more fixed point, such as the gates of a city. Variety in the suggestion of places on the Elizabethan stage was given by these doors, the balcony, the tower above the balcony, and the proscenium, a variety still more developed by the use of curtains, which when closed generally implied an indoor scene in which the curtain represented the arras : revealing, when it was opened, an inner room. Peele, Marlowe, and Webster made use of this device as well as Shakespeare.[1] It seems probable that curtains were freely used to mask scenes which were being prepared with cumbrous properties, just as, in a modern theatre, the act-drop is used for the same purpose. In *Antony and Cleopatra,* where the balcony is used as the " monument," the audience would see it from without, and the scene of Antony's death within the " monument" would be enacted on the stage below.[2]

When we add to our knowledge of the devices of the Elizabethan stage that of the numerous properties and stage furniture which helped to produce the illusion of a throne-room or a camp, it is clear that the setting of the Elizabethan stage made a double appeal to the audience. There was the division of the stage into concrete parts in which different scenes could be acted, there was also the possibility of still further localizing the scenes by signs or notices, by stage furniture, and by references in the dialogue. The possibilities of staging a complicated plot were almost unrivalled. In the plays themselves we trace a double appeal : the reference to a historical or legendary plot, with all its traditional implications, and the concentration, within the plot, on the portrayal of individual character.

Mr. William Poel, who did so much to revive Elizabethan dramatic staging, has drawn attention to the alternation of groups of actors who relieved one another

[1] See R. Crompton Rhodes, *The Stagery of Shakespeare,* p. 26 *et seq.*
[2] *Ibid.,* pp. 62, 63.

on the stage. At the same time, Shakespearean critics have become increasingly aware of the peculiar character of the plots of Elizabethan plays, by which interest is alternately gained for the public and private life of the hero, or for his earthly life and his influence after death, or for two sides of his character— the crisis marking the moment when we are made most fully aware of this double movement, or when some external event or agency helps to declare it. There is here a most evident case of interaction between stage technique and plot-construction, which may be illustrated from almost any Elizabethan play.[1] Too strong a contrast between two types of action, or plot and underplot, is obviated by a pervading atmosphere of enchantment as in *A Midsummer Night's Dream*, or of war in the Roman and historical plays, or of the " vendetta " in *Romeo and Juliet*. In this atmosphere events and characters which might seem over-emphatic find their place.

Simple examples of the use made by Shakespeare of the two groups of actors, the one more serious, the other suggesting comic relief, and always emerging from different sides of the actors' house, can be seen in the *Merchant of Venice, A Midsummer Night's Dream*, and *The Tempest*.

In a more complicated play such as *Hamlet*, we find Hamlet associated with many groups of actors, and here it is the hero who supplies in his own person a good deal of the general magnetic atmosphere, or at any rate is the means of transmitting it to the audience. To take an example from the historical plays, Prince Henry collects the riotous actors round him in *Henry IV*, and in *Henry V* is the centre of serious action. In *Julius Cæsar* the influence of

---

[1] The parts also were frequently doubled.

Cæsar in the main action is continued after his fall, and the cleavage in the play is that between the outer and inner lives of the personages. Different scenes bring along with them different actors, according to whether the emphasis is on public or private life.

The form of the theatre, too, directs the position of the crisis. The French stage could have a situation closed at once by the drop of the curtain, as in a modern play : and the tendency was to work up to a crisis and then shut off the world of romance. But the Elizabethans had to get off their stage as best they could. And thus Shakespeare, master of his craft, nearly always brings on the minor characters at the end of the play to effect the transition from the tragedy, or the romance, to common life. So men came in to bear off the bodies in *Hamlet* and in *Lear*. In the *Merchant of Venice* the episode of the rings concludes the play after the excitement of the Trial scene is over. The alternation of scenes in a Shakespearean play was not only useful in practice, as giving a rest to each set of actors, it also meant that the chief incidents, though separated by appreciable intervals, were staged in such a way as to prevent the audience from anticipating the working out of the plot, for between the great scenes the audience was occupied with secondary matters.

The performance of Masques in the sixteenth and seventeenth centuries (we have an early instance in *The Tempest*) brought in a spectacular element that led very rapidly to the introduction of scenery and operatic effect. Attention was withdrawn from the problems of character to effects of grouping, and the need for scenery and music was immediately felt. The history of the stage in this particular is similar in England and on the Continent.

With the desire for effect, the proscenium began to shrink, and the stage filled in to the boxes. Thus in a modern theatre there is a frame for the characters, and a kind of artistic remoteness is produced, and a new effect which is different from the realistic conception of drama as felt by the Elizabethans. Our London theatres are a compromise, in plan, between the Elizabethan system and the modern desire for spectacular effect and romantic remoteness. The neutral ground of the proscenium, so important in Greek and mediæval drama, has completely disappeared.

A study of the plays of the Elizabethan period illustrates very remarkably the fact that though the force of that drama lies in complicated action rather than, as in the Greek stage, in simple action, the two essential elements of stage production, viz. a neutral space for action, and significance of character-drawing, are represented in both dramas together with an enveloping dramatic atmosphere.

The Elizabethan drama was at its full strength in the first quarter of the seventeenth century: and the work of Shakespeare was surrounded by that of many other dramatists, who wrote, as he did, with a view to the conditions of the Elizabethan stage. Some few dramatists who just preceded Shakespeare belonged to the group of Oxford and Cambridge men who had been concerned with the presentation of plays (mainly derived from Seneca, though sometimes of Biblical and sometimes of Italian origin) in the college halls of the universities. The staging of these plays was simple: a platform was built up at the end of the hall removed from the high table, and the existing doors and musicians' gallery were used for the actors' exits and entrances. The same plan applied to plays given in the Guildhall and other city halls.[1]

Of Shakespeare's contemporaries the most important is Ben Jonson, not only on account of his remarkable output, including such a masterpiece as *The Alchemist*, with its characters drawn from the life of London, but also on account of the variety found in his work. The masques which he developed into a definite " genre " with spectacular music and dancing led to experiments such as Milton's *Comus* at a later date.

Among Shakespeare's contemporaries and successors the heroic couplet and blank verse were both used for tragedy, and prose for the comedies. The tragedies soon show signs of decadence : the ghostly apparitions in Chapman's, Marston's, and Tourneur's plays are frequent and concrete, and introduced with a lavish use of language. The call to revenge, which struck the imagination of the readers of Seneca's versions of the *Œdipus* and the *Agamemnon* and was apparent in an earlier *Hamlet* as well as in Shakespeare's play, was the motive for the intrusion of the unseen world into these dramas of violent action. Webster aims at producing an atmosphere of presage and fear more than at the concrete exhibition of a terror-striking ghost ; and on the other hand he admits musical dirges into his plays. The opposition of Puritanism to stage production, which began to be evident about 1630, was about to culminate in the Civil War and Puritan Revolution which cut short the dramatic tradition in England till after the Restoration.[2]

[1] There was, however, an instance of more elaborate scenery in Christ Church Hall in 1605 when James I visited the University, and elaborate stage-arrangements were designed by Inigo Jones. See Lamborn and Harrison, *Shakespeare, the Man and His Stage*.

[2] In 1625 all theatres were closed on account of the plague : they were opened again in 1637, when the plague had abated, but officially closed through Puritan influence in 1642.

CHAPTER IV

FROM THE RENAISSANCE TO NEO-CLASSICISM

IN considering the history of the stage from the Renaissance to the neo-classic period, we have to compare the methods of stage production in comedy and tragedy. In comedy, Spain and France produced a tradition that was independent of Roman influence. Both in Spain and France this new tradition was initiated by the strolling players who acted popular comedy. The strolling players in Italy, too, produced their independent method in the comedy of masks. In the three countries theatrical practice hardened into very different forms. It will be convenient in examining them to begin with Spain in the sixteenth century, and then consider Italy and France in the seventeenth and eighteenth.

Spanish dramatic art, as we have said, was little affected by Seneca's plays, because Spain possessed a free form of national drama, curiously like that of the Elizabethans in England.[1] Spain had its very strong provincial characteristics, and national and Christian feeling had been aroused by the long conflict with the Moors without destroying local character. Spain, too, was a primitive country, possessing large mountain districts and few and scattered towns. In

[1] But in the Jesuit schools, as in France, the boys performed Latin plays.

the towns the technical industries were important, and the kind of audience collected at a play included the bourgeoisie, shopkeepers, and artisans, as well as the land-owning classes. Such an audience enjoyed a realistic description of life, and plenty of action in the drama. Lope de Vega's plays (of which there was an immense output) satisfied both conditions. His drama had a romantic background and played fast and loose with geography, chronology, and general likelihood very much as Shakespeare's had done. He described foreigners of all types and they were all through intensely Spanish. His plays were staged in the courtyard or *patio* of a great house, a rough platform being put at one end. From the windows and balconies ladies could look on, but they were not supposed to appear below. A rough farce was frequently added to the more serious comedy to please the " mosqueteros " (groundlings) who stood in the courtyard. It was probably also as a concession to them that independent farcical scenes were added after the first act and ballets after the second and third. The Spanish drama was divided into acts or *days*, and the division was marked by an interlude. In such a primitive form of staging no scenery was used, and the properties were of the simplest. This simplicity of presentation, natural to the touring companies of the sixteenth century, lasted into the seventeenth century, when Calderon's plays were acted. The Spanish play was unencumbered by stage devices of any kind. Where, as in Calderon's *The Constant Prince*, a supernatural army comes in, it appears on the stage as a real army, and is not summoned from the " vasty deep " below the stage-line. Two chairs, a gallows, a window and balcony, cloaks and masks were the simple *mise-en-scène*. Stage crowds, scenery, and music were not used until in the national decadence of the eighteenth century dramatic ideas were borrowed from France, and the classic tradition was introduced. The plays themselves, apart from the interludes, were short. Unlike the Elizabethan play, which has at the beginning slight scenes in which minor characters introduce the subject of the play, the Spanish play begins with a monologue in order to introduce the actors and prepare the way for the plot. In the seventeenth century these monologues gave a poetical dramatist his opportunity for lyrical verse and elevation of feeling.

The religious tendency of the Spanish mind, and the preoccupation felt with the underlying problems of life and death, in a world superficially gay and full of absorption in things of the senses, led the dramatic author to present his ideas in a dual form. The abstract morality was put into a shape for presentation in a church as a religious act or *auto*; the lay version for the strolling players shows the story worked out in ordinary life. Only in Spain do we have this constant doubling of a dramatic idea. The result of working at a play in two ways is to bring considerable experience and criticism to bear on it; and the form of a play in Spain, its movement from the beginning to the *dénouement*, is beyond all praise. One kind of play, too, the religious act or *auto*, affected the more concrete form of the story and vice versa. In the seventeenth century we find Calderon greatly influenced, as the title of one of his plays bears witness, by the temporary and dream-like character of human life, expressing this even in the lay play *El vida es Sueño (Life's a Dream)*, in the corresponding *auto*, and in other plays. This is, from one point of view, a realistic treatment of the drama, as it brings the experience of the audience close to that of the characters in the play.

In the Spanish " cloak and sword " comedies of the sixteenth century we have the pith of Spanish popular drama. The action is extremely rapid ; words are immediately followed by blows and blows by some sudden intervention that closes the play.[1] In the Spanish play the king, especially the contemporary one, is the *Deus ex machina* and controls the issues of the plot. He has as many disguises as the Caliph in the Arabian Nights' story, and uses them to the same good purpose, to know his people.

A seventeenth-century French audience, accustomed to the Spanish plays which were frequently to be seen in Paris during the days of Louis XIII and Louis XIV, would be in no way surprised at the intervention of the king at the close of *Tartuffe*, for this was a very mild expedient in contrast with the methods of Spanish comedy, as can be seen if we compare with *Tartuffe* the Spanish *El Alcalde di Zalamea*, where the king comes in person to hold a court of justice and conclude the play.

The part played by Fate in a Greek tragedy was taken in Spain by the laws of honour, which controlled human action and destiny.[2] The king, as we have seen, was placed in the position of God, and sometimes was able to deal with the problem of the demands of honour and the needs of the individual life. We see this atmosphere strongly reflected in Corneille's *Cid*.

The effect of the Spanish influence on the staging of Molière's plays is very important. He adopts the plan of ballets and " entrées " of different kinds to

[1] Some aspects of the " cloak and sword " comedy are parodied by Sir Andrew Aguecheek and Sir Toby Belch in *Twelfth Night*.

[2] In later fate-dramas, such as the *Maréchale d'Ancre*, destiny is the " troisième personnage." In many modern plays the idea of heredity takes this place, as in *Les Avariés*.

give variety to his lighter comedies, but tends gradually to incorporate the movement in the plot, until he gets a unity of plan instead of a comedy with disjointed interludes.   The fact that in Spain people could come freely in to a play had caused the drama to appeal to the popular interest : and for that reason the interludes became necessary.   In France where the audience was of a more intellectual type a consistent play was desired.

Molière owed a great deal, especially in his early work, to the traditional French farce, of which examples are found from the thirteenth century onwards.   From the fanciful plays of Adam de la Halle (*Le jeu d'Adam, Robin et Marion*) to the story of *Maître Pathelin*, and in the group of plays contemporary with the latter, the old French farce was noticeable for its shrewd reflection of life and manners.   It always possessed the humour which is derived from observation, whether of a kindly or a harsh nature.   The setting of such plays was simple, as the whole interest was thrown on the interaction of character.   The costumes were those of the period.   In these ways the farce differed from the " sotie," which had a political aim and in which types appeared.   This use of types and abstract characters necessitated symbolic dress to bring out the meaning of the figures.

There is then a twofold development of the secular play in France which differs from the development of the folk play in Italy.   In Italy folk drama inevitably seemed to retain the character of the old Roman Saturnine play.   Masks and dumb-show and a plot and dialogue that grew out of the contact of certain familiar comic figures were characteristic of the " commedia dell' Arte."

In Italy, national drama was, as in Spain, provincial in character, and apart from the tragedies and opera presented in the larger theatres, popular plays were of the nature of farce, the actors belonging to a travelling company and picking up ideas of types and characterization as they went along. In the Italian comedy-of-masks we should notice (1) the use of *patois* or dialect in defining a character and its local origin ; (2) the use of the square or street as a neutral place for the action of the play. Thus when the strolling players possessed a theatre and scenery the latter was constructed on the Roman model but developed in a simpler form to represent the familiar piazza surrounded by houses. A solid building occupied the right and left of the stage, with windows, doors, and a balcony. Behind was a street, or a bridge, and a drop-scene. It was perfectly natural in Italian comedy to represent all action as taking place in the square, with exits and entrances to houses. When, however, the scenery was used by Molière on the alternate days when he occupied the Salle du Petit Bourbon, he was obliged to arrange his play in such a way as to fit in with the Italian setting. Thus he makes his doctors consult in the street, an unusual performance : wills are made there and lovers' appointments are held in the same place.[1] Molière makes his characters constantly refer to the happy accident of a meeting which saves the trouble of going indoors. This Italian stage was very difficult to light, and as the proscenium projected, the French characters were in the habit of coming forward and standing near the edge of the stage. Molière's characters therefore stand nearly all through the plays, though in necessary cases (as in *Le Malade imaginaire*) a chair is brought forward, and in *Tartuffe* a table with a cloth.

As the French stage was lighted by lamps in the place of footlights, the position in front was the best

[1] See *M. de Pourceaugnac* and *L'Ecole des Maris.*

lighted. This lighting by lamps had been necessary on the French stage because the old tennis-courts near the walls of Paris were the first fixed theatres. These courts had a platform, but very high windows through which little light came, and more had to be supplied.[1] The narrow platform was shut off by a curtain, which could close a dramatic performance without delay.

The habit of wandering players was to speak very loudly, even to rant, and to use a great deal of gesture. Shakespeare alludes to this tearing of a passion to tatters at the hands of strolling players.[2] In France the rough platforms on which Hardy's plays were acted in the sixteenth century were very high—nine to twelve feet above the ground—and at that distance voices carried with difficulty and much gesture had to be used. This over-emphasis had to be curbed by the great dramatists of the seventeenth century. On the outdoor stage soliloquy was frequently used to bring the audience into touch with what was going on. This was less necessary indoors, but was still the habit in France in the seventeenth century, where the actors were remote from the audience.[3] In tragedy, however, the remoteness was not broken through, and the characters addressed one another.

[1] The size was approximately 100 × 46 feet = a measurement of a medium-sized college dining-hall in one of the older British universities.

[2] " O, it offends me to the soul to hear a robustious periwig-pated fellow tear a passion to tatters, to very rags, to split the ears of the groundlings. . . ."—*Hamlet*, Act III, sc. 2.

[3] In the " tragedy of blood " of the sixteenth century in France the play did not end with the crisis : after-events were detailed before the conclusion of the drama. When plays were acted indoors, in the seventeenth century, the crisis marked the end of the play, and the curtains were drawn.

The history of stage scenery in French drama of the seventeenth century has an interest of its own. The practice of the mediæval stage had been to provide for what is known as the "simultaneous setting," in which different parts of the stage could be used for different scenes.[1] This practice survived at any rate up to 1637, for the plays by Corneille and by' Mairet up to that date required the mediæval setting for an adequate production of the plays.[2] We have evidence that certain modifications were made in the stage decoration of this period to simplify the arrangements; for instance, Mairet's *Criséide et Arimate* needed a tomb and altar in one act only, and they were only placed on the stage for that time.[2] Or again curtains were opened to "disclose" a new scene,[2] where on the mediæval stage they were only used to mask actions "off" the stage. But the practice had to yield entirely in course of time to the new and simple setting which was employed for the later plays of Corneille and for Racine's tragedies, because the mediæval system conflicted with the feeling in the neo-classic writers for a unity of space. Thus dramatic theory affected stage-production in the seventeenth century. This point may be illustrated by an account of the two performances of Corneille's *Le Cid*. In 1637 it was produced with a simultaneous setting ; but in 1682 the stage only contained a "palais à volonté." An intervening method was suggested by La Mesnardière,[3] who advised that an "écriteau" should be put up, as it is

---

[1] See the plan of the Valenciennes passion play, frontispiece.
[2] See D. C. Stuart, *Stage Decoration and the Unity of Place in France in the Seventeenth Century* (*Modern Philology*), Vol. X, No. 3.
[3] *La poétique*, Paris, 1640.

commonly reported to have been on the Elizabethan stage, to define the "lieu théâtral" more closely with reference to the text.[1] D'Aubignac, in his *Pratique du Théâtre,* more clearly adheres to the unity of place, but advises the use of curtains where necessary, for concealment or "disclosures." It appears to be likely that the need for some modification in the setting brought about the habit of dropping the curtain between the acts, when music was used to disguise the noise made by the rearrangement of the stage. A study of the plays of the seventeenth century shows that some amount of change in scenery was only reluctantly abandoned.

In one case, however, instead of the modification of practice by theory, we have a modification of theory by practice. Molière first played before the King and Court in the Salle des Gardes in the Louvre. Later he was allowed to use the "Salle du Petit Bourbon,"[2] and when his troupe performed before the King at Versailles, the setting was at first intended to give as nearly as possible the effect of the "Salle." Folding screens, painted to represent the walls with doors and windows of the original room, were transferred to any room set apart in the palace for the purpose, and the arrangement provided for the necessary exits and entrances. Further practice, however, modified this custom.

[1] "Nous permettons aux Dramatiques d'étendre en ces occasions les bornes de leur Théâtre et de partager leur Scène en plusieurs cartiers différens, pourveu qu'ils y fassent écrire, *Cet endroit figure le Louvre,* et *Cy est la Place Royale.*"

[2] A contemporary engraving shows the flattened archway which framed the scenes, approached from the "salle" by a flight of steps, the galleries round the hall for the use of spectators, and the lighting of the hall itself by heavy candelabra. See Karl Mantzius, *History of Theatrical Art,* Vol. IV.

When Molière helped in the production of plays for the great royal carnival known as *Les plaisirs de l'Ile Enchanté*, the plays were acted out of doors in the part of the palace gardens that seemed most suitable. So, for example, *Psyche* had several scenes : the " Grotte d'Apollon " was made to serve for the gates of hell, and when the scene was changed to a lake or formal garden, the audience moved to the new place chosen in the grounds. Thus changes of scene were introduced on the stage, and when Molière had his next plays acted within doors, his screens were painted with realistic trees and sky, columns and rocks and temples. The advent of the opera developed this into modern scenery.

The staging of tragedy in the seventeenth century in France was relatively simple. The more closely the interest of the play was concentrated the less need there was to invoke scenic effect. The theory of the drama and its general appeal is thus more important than the staging. But we know that artificial light was used where footlights are placed on a modern stage, and that a curtain was drawn to indicate the end of a play. It is also known that the French were affected by classical tradition in the matter of the means used to awake pity and terror. In Greek and Roman plays murders were represented behind the acting stage, and in the Greek theatre doors were opened and the body of the slain person brought out and exhibited on the stage. (This can be illustrated from Sophocles' *Agamemnon*.) The French accepted the necessity for a similar restraint, more especially as they had adopted the method of placing the crisis at the end of a play since the establishment of fixed theatres. Hardy's " tragedy of blood " in the preceding century more closely resembled the Elizabethan tragic drama. Hence the French theorists of the

seventeenth century in France, claiming that by
enforcing the classical tradition they had improved
upon earlier methods, criticized the continuance of
this method among English dramatists of the seventeenth century in England.[1] D'Aubignac, together
with all French critics, was opposed, in the interests
of tradition, order, and moderation, to the crowding
of the stage with action that could have been reported,
to spectacular effect as such, and in fact to anything
which tended to confuse his main idea that unity of
place should be kept, and that the stage was the
place for dramatic action essential to the plot, and
neither for decoration nor for side issues.

Towards the end of the seventeenth century these
criticisms produced an effect on England, and the
murders on the English stage were partially concealed,
and the result explained by a " discovery."[2]

Corneille's tragedies, in so many ways reminiscent
of classical Greek plays, were simply staged. So were
Racine's, and here the narrow stage tended to draw
the audience into the fully-charged emotional atmosphere of the play. Where, however, Racine wrote
for outdoor performance, as in *Esther* and *Athalie*,
he used changes of scene, and put allusions to natural
scenery into these two last plays. Corneille's plays
had the character of a rather grandiose recitation, for
which the only need was a neutral space. Racine's
plays invoke not so much the spaces where Divine
thought and human life can interact, as the narrowest
limits within which a passionate conflict can be fought

[1] See, in particular, d'Aubignac's *Pratique du Théâtre*, 1657,
translated into English in 1684.

[2] See Settle's *Conquest of China by the Tartars*, produced
1674, and Banks's *The Destruction of Troy*, produced 1678,
for the use of the " discovery " or uncovering of a scene
showing the result of a murder. See on these points L. B.
Campbell, *Scenes and Machines on the English Stage.*

out ; and the sense of distance and mystery which
he unquestionably introduces, is due to the presence
in the atmosphere of what Maeterlinck calls the
" troisième personnage "—fate, or Divine life, or
human life in general—which reacts on the individual
protagonist and antagonist. This " troisième personnage " is, Maeterlinck thinks, " a necessity to
tragedy." Ancient Greece had her Nemesis, Spain her
laws of honour, Elizabethan England her sense of an
unseen world which explained human conditions :
Corneille had the hand of God controlling past and
future, and offering the gift of eternal life to the tragic
hero who conquered himself though betrayed by circumstances. This third element, definite with Corneille,
was mysterious with Racine, and appeared occasionally
in symbolic form.

It is in complete accordance with the new method of
Racine's art that he illustrates the unconscious as well
as the conscious processes of the mind. In French
tragedy before his time, and especially in the work
of Corneille, there had been an attempt to express as
completely as possible the character and actions of
the persons in the drama. This was done through
clear and comprehensive speeches, intended to convey
all that was necessary for the development of the
plot. Racine, claiming more fully than Corneille the
co-operation of the actor with the dramatist, gave
frequent opportunities to the cast for the suggestion
of thoughts and emotions half-recognized by the
characters themselves, or sometimes not acknowledged
at all by them. These are thoughts and emotions
that have not yet emerged into action, or even into
expression in words, and yet form the groundwork
on which the action of the play is gradually built up.
It is evident that great dramatic effects could be introduced through this use of one of the everyday experi-

ences of human intercourse.   But to render the effect
upon the stage calls upon the best powers of the inter-
preters of the play : the dramatist gives them an
opportunity but cannot supply a complete formula
of expression.   Thus the actor in Racine's plays
has a share that is crucial in the creation of a
part.[1]

Again, in another way, the actors took their share
in the expression of the dramatist's idea. When
Racine's plays were performed, it was no longer obliga-
tory on the actors to stand in a rigid row and declaim
their lines, each character listening in turn with silent
attention to the rest. The habit of recitation usual
in the performances of Corneille's plays was disappear-
ing from the stage, and Racine's plays were written
for the new mode. Each actor, when not uttering
his lines, could allow what was being said to influence

---

[1] Examples of the emergence of the unacknowledged
impulse are frequent in Racine's plays, and in many cases,
such as that of the development of cruelty in Néron (*Britanni-
cus*, Act II, sc. 2, lines 521–6, *Ibid.*, sc. 3, lines 679–84, *Ibid.*,
Act III, sc. 2, lines 800–8, *Ibid.*, Act IV, sc. 3, lines 1332–6
et passim), this is itself the main psychological interest of
the play, and must be so interpreted by the actors : but
there are other cases where the working of the impulse is
only suggested fitfully, in occasional glimpses. A striking
example occurs in *Iphigénie*, where Agamemnon loses the
thread of his speech with Arcas, and unconsciously utters
his fear of his own half-expressed decision to slay his daughter.
(Act I, sc. 1, line 40.)   "Non, tu ne mourras point, je n'y
puis consentir."   This passage occurs at the opening of the
play, and at once produces an atmosphere of tragic doubt.
An almost similar line in *Andromaque* acquaints us with the
result of the queen's mental struggles. Other examples
occur in *Phèdre*, as, for example, in the dialogue between
the queen and Cenone, Act III, sc. 8, line 1036 :
" Dieux ! que ne suis-je assise à l'ombre des forêts !
Quand pourrai-je, au travers d'une noble poussière,
Suivre de l'œil un char fuyant dans la carrière."

him visibly, through gesture and expression.[1] Thus
in Racine's plays, the silence of the actors could be
eloquent, and the art of the stage gained a new opportunity in tragedy. Similar opportunities had been
freely used in comedy, where pantomimic gesture
helped to carry on the action of the piece,[2] but freedom
of expressive gestures had not been used so early in
tragedy. Racine is said to have studied the effects,
and possibilities of effect, in his scenes by reciting
plays aloud as he was composing or modifying them.
Thus we hear that he repeated passages of *Mithridate*
aloud when walking in the Tuileries : and it is well
known that he studied the parts in the plays with the
actors : thus setting a tradition of interpretation
which has been a continuous one.

But, it may be said, in whatever way Racine collected
and used his material, he attained an effect which is
nearer to that of the Greek tragic drama than that
of any other master of the dramatic art. This is a
view that can be justified, without, however, implying
any large degree of imitation of Greek methods. For
Racine was able to construct his plays on such simple
lines that their form suggests an analogy with Greek

[1] Although this is part of the actor's art, it is a part more
fully cultivated in the Latin races than in the more northern
nations of Europe. Expression is there less limited to facial
expression, and in all Latin races there is a natural response
of the whole body to the stimulus of emotion.

[2] The performance of farces in the streets, where from the
position of the actors on the boards and the general circumstances spoken words would not carry well, tended to
develop in comedy other means of expression. The history
of Italian comedy, which greatly influenced French seventeenth-century comedy, pointed to considerable use of action
on the stage ; the words in the case of the Italian players being
sometimes left to the invention of the actor, who could in
any case vary them at will. In England the Elizabethan
dumb-show and mummers' plays, which were traditional,
put similar emphasis on action and gesture.

drama. As he has also drawn his characters imaginatively from real experience, there is nothing archaic or aloof from life in his setting of the stories. The appeal to a French audience was as direct as the appeal to Greek onlookers in the days of Euripides, and this point is emphasized by Racine himself in the preface to *Iphigénie*.[1]

Again, while he avoids the actual participation of supernatural beings in the action (here he diverges from Greek practice, though less so from that of Euripides than from that of the other two great tragedians), he conveys a sense of the power of unseen forces, and he does this in a spirit that is certainly Greek, by causing these forces to act along the lines of natural events and catastrophes. Thus in *Phèdre* the sea-monster and the gigantic wave translate the will of Neptune and destroy Hippolyte.[2] In *Iphigénie* the Divine anger is felt in the calm of the seas and the paralysis of movement,[3] and the relaxing of the spell is recognized when the gods accept the sacrifice of Eriphile with fire from heaven.[4] In the remaining plays we have allusions to the hand of the gods, as compelling human fate in a secret and mysterious way, for example, in *Bérénice*, where Titus explains his persistent misfortunes in this way.[5] In *Esther* and *Athalie* Racine recognizes good and evil supernatural

----

[1] " Le goût de Paris s'est trouvé conforme à celui d'Athènes, mes spectateurs ont été émus des mêmes choses qui ont mis autrefois en larmes le plus savant peuple de la Grèce, et qui ont fait dire qu'entre les poètes Euripides étoit extrêmement tragique, τραγικώτατος, c'est à dire qu'il savoit merveilleusement exciter la compassion et la terreur, qui sont les véritables effets de la tragédie."

[2] *Phèdre*, Act V, sc. 6, lines 1498–1570.
[3] *Iphigénie*, Act I, sc. 1, lines 7–9.
[4] *Iphigénie*, Act V, sc. 6, lines 1777–90.
[5] *Bérénice*, Act V, sc. 7, lines 1407–14.

agencies, and believes in the ultimate triumph of good. The characters in these plays live in the clear light of that knowledge : the " sense of God " fills the temple of *Athalie*, the temple which is here the antechamber to the Holy of holies.

Racine suggests, in all his plays, the existence of hereditary forces which bind the different generations together, and account for some of the interplay of passion to be observed. For the first time in the history of French literature he creates the doctrine that any action that can be explained in this way is thereby excused. Thus Racine sets going a current which can be seen in its full strength in the romantic novel of the nineteenth century.[1] The appeal of *Phèdre*, for example, is not only one which excites pity for the tragedy of the individual life : it also rouses sympathy for the woman who is betrayed by her own hereditary instincts. Fate has conspired with passion to destroy her self-control and the confusion of motives causes all blame to be drowned in pity.

Racine has also used but has modified other conditions that are essential to a Greek plot. One of these, in the Greek drama, is the presentation of some problem of feeling or conduct which affects the society described in the play. This problem is then not isolated in the life of an individual human being. Such problems occur, for example, in the *Antigone* and in *Œdipus Rex*. Racine shows a similar problem of conduct, but in his plays the problem has to be solved by a hero or heroine who is at the same time exasperated by some passionate emotion which destroys strength of will. Only in *Andromaque* does the central character retain enough power over her action to keep the problem of conduct on the level of a Greek play, though

[1] The doctrine was re-stated by Rousseau, and influenced first the novel and then the stage.

in *Phèdre* there is more than a suggestion of this kind of conflict. *Athalie* is, in this sense, more Greek than the plays formed on Greek models. Another essential mark of a Greek tragedy in its early form is concerned with the amount of action which takes place on the stage. The custom seems to have been that the events which immediately surrounded the central conflict should be seen in actual process in the play or group of plays to be acted. For a Greek play which formed part of a trilogy was organically connected with the other parts. The historical events alluded to or remembered or reflected upon by the chorus in the central play had great weight with an audience that had just seen these events acted : while the consequences of a central action were destined themselves to be seen later on in dramatic form. Where, as occasionally happened in the drama of Euripides, the play did not form part of a trilogy, the dramatist made an effort to place on the stage everything that was necessary for the development of his own dramatic idea. Racine's method lies between the two. He makes use of the monologues and long speeches of his characters to put the audience into possession of their inner history, and thus suggests the background of historical experience, which has not been described in any previous play in direct connexion with it, and therefore is not so vividly present to the mind of the spectator as it was in the case of the onlookers at a Greek drama. The monologues in Racine's plays then acquire considerable importance ; and so do his narrative speeches.

There is a gulf between the earlier plays of Racine and the two later plays, *Esther* and *Athalie*, where the struggle is not between passion and fate, but between good and evil, and where the victory of good is assured. The tragic abandonment of human wills to an evil destiny has been succeeded by a faith in the sure foundations of the world.

This belief in the beauty and triumph of goodness has affected the allusions to nature and to natural scenes—few though they are—which occur in the later plays. Before *Esther* and *Athalie* the whole interest of the plays was a psychological one; the extreme violence of the central action allowing no respite for the attention of the spectator. The natural background, where alluded to, was a place of fear and mystery. So Phèdre mentions the dim forests as a place where shame and passion could be hidden,[1] and the characters in *Iphigénie* are conscious of the surrounding silence of the air, and then of the final release.[2] But in *Esther* and *Athalie* the mind is set free to love and admire the beauty of the setting : in the former play we have definite indications of the place and character of each scene : in the latter, beautiful effects of light [3] and the sense of the ordered solemnity of the Temple services, and the movement of the vast crowds which are concerned in the play, together with allusions to the valleys and brooks and the distant desert beyond them.[4] Thus the art of Racine does not exclude an

[1] *Phèdre*, Act I, sc. 3, lines 176–8 :
   " Dieu ! que ne suis-je assise à l'ombre des forêts."
Ibid., Act IV, sc. 6, lines 1236 :
   " Dans le fond des forêts alloient-ils se cacher ? "
[2] *Iphigénie*, Act I, sc. 1, lines 8–9 :
   " Les vents nous auroient-ils exaucés cette nuit ?
   Mais tout dort, et l'armée, et les vents, et Neptune."
Ibid., sc. 2, line 201 :
   " Du silence des vents demandez-leur la cause."
Ibid., Act V, sc. 6, lines 1779–80 :
   " Les vents agissent l'air d'heureux frémissements,
   Et la mer leur répond par ses mugissements. . . ."
[3] E.g., in *Athalie*, Act I, sc. 1, line 160 :
   " Et du temple déjà l'aube blanchit le faîte."
[4] *Athalie*, Act III, sc. 6.

interest in nature, but the action is so concentrated in his earlier plays that it would have been a fault in art to divert the attention of the audience from the psychological problem ; and it is only in the last two plays that the more mature philosophy of life they express issues in greater freedom of the spirit of man, and a closer relation to God and the world.

In the study of the tragedy of the seventeenth century in France a comparison suggests itself between the work of Racine and that of Corneille. However clearly we see the two great writers in their historical relation to one another, we cannot consider Racine's art merely as a development of Corneille's. It was, for his own time, a new art of the drama. The interest of Corneille's plays is in the theory of life which they propound ; and the heroic scale on which action is produced for judgment. There is a warm current, too, of romantic feeling in the plays, which though specially noticeable in *Le Cid* also helps the movement of the tragedies. The women, Pauline and Emilie for instance, have heroic parts to play, but they also have very human temperaments. Thus the situations created by Corneille's plots are as a rule dealt with in a way that is convincing and natural ; having regard to the fact that the plots centre in a great conflict, in the crisis of which men and women rise above themselves, and do this with " conscious, clear-eyed endurance." The issue is of the simple and splendid kind that is consoling to humanity, showing, as it does, of what humanity is capable.[1]

[1] Although there is little in common between the crafts-manship of Shakespeare and that of Corneille, there is a great likeness in the appeal made by both writers to the Divine quality in human nature, and similar problems of conscience and will, similar questionings about the parts of fate or

And in the process of martyrdom for a cause, not only do complex issues become simple, but pain vanishes both for the hero and for the spectator. The choice is made, the will is triumphant, and suffering is turned to joy. But the drama of Racine does not aim at exciting an atmosphere in which admiration of the spiritual possibilities of man is the main and essential element. It desires to quicken a power in the spectators to feel and realize the possibilities of tragedy in lives like their own, but presented with all the romantic detachment of stage conditions. Thus, while the plot, the historical allusions and the names of the characters are frequently traditional, the painting of emotional situation is true to contemporary life, and full of realistic detail.[1] In this way Racine dispenses to a great extent with passages in his plays which give an external historical narration of facts; the psychological states of the characters are in close connexion with the development of the plot, and convince the spectators by their likelihood and their parallel with ordinary experience. The expression of Hermione's jealousy, of Orestes' exasperated insight

chance in human life, have occurred both to the French and English dramatists. While Shakespeare creates a number of characters that belong to everyday experience, he succeeds in placing his heroes on a different plane.

" Has not Shakespeare himself hinted that his figures are partly mythologic and partly symbolic when he withdraws them so far from the everyday world. Why is Prospero placed on a magic island ? Why are Hamlet and Macbeth and Lear all withdrawn into a remote and almost legendary past ? Even Othello, who is much more like an ordinary human being, is still set apart as if he were a symbolic figure by his blackness."—*Hamlet and the Scottish Succession*, by L. Winstanley, p. 27.

[1] The attack in the eighteenth century on the classical stage of the seventeenth is not justified by facts, for the plays of Racine led naturally to the development of feeling as shown in eighteenth-century *drame*.

into her motives, of the violent though simple emotion of Pyrrhus, and of the gathering strength of Andromaque's decision—to mention only one play—is obtained by the methods which are easy to recognize but are the effect of great art ; the words chosen are elementary and clear, but fit exactly into the context of feeling and thus convey an impression of truth to life.   Racine thus differs from Corneille in the effect he produces as well as in the method of dramatic detachment of which he makes use.   The form, too, that of the poetical drama, in which no great contrasts of diction are allowed, is more perfectly defined than that of Corneille, and becomes in Racine's hands an instrument the very restraints of which help to intensify the underlying effects of emotion.   It is clear then that we cannot describe Racine's drama in the terms of Corneille's.

The art of the tragic drama, though presenting in the work of Corneille and Racine a problem of moral conflict, is then capable of very different forms of expression.   This is even more evident when the whole subject of dramatic art is considered historically. It may be convenient now to sum up the many views on the tragic drama and its expression up to the end of the neo-classic period.

We cannot limit our conception of tragedy to that of the conflict of the individual will—in which case Corneille's would show the typical tragic spirit—for the interest of tragedy lies also in defining the kind of conflict, and in the arena of consciousness in which it is fought out.   There is thus room for many types of tragedy, including ancient and modern forms as distinct as those, for example, of Æschylus, Shakespeare, and Racine.

In the Æschylean trilogy, the hero of any one part of the play is not necessarily aware of the meaning of the conflict in which he is engaged.   His consciousness is often imperfect and the meaning of the struggle only comes out when it has affected more than one generation. Thus in the *Agamemnon* the characters are driven by forces which are only explained by family history, and have to find their solution in a later play. Sophocles indeed made each play an artistic whole, but even so the dramatic situation still depends for its meaning on a knowledge of the family history. Sophocles makes a dramatic use of the gradual wakening of his heroes to hereditary sin and its consequences ; but Œdipus, though he shares in hereditary crime, is more the individual hero of the one play than is the central figure in a play by Æschylus. The drama of Greece began as a picture of the consciousness of a family in time, and became a study of the individual with a responsibility for hereditary sin or wrongs. With Euripides the consciousness was still more localized, as, for example, in the case of Medea and Phædra ; the evil which attacked them came as a temptation to their own character and temperament. When the unit of the play ceased to be the family, more stress was laid on the notion of individual conflict, and thus the struggle became more poignant and as it were inseparable from the life of a tragic hero. It is true that in a later age, for example in the Elizabethan period, we find the consciousness shared by contemporary persons, and thus " group actions " are produced (as in some of Shakespeare's historical plays). And it is sometimes suggested that the spirit of the nation shares in the conflict.[1] In modern drama either an individual or a group has the consciousness of the issues at stake.[2] But in Shakespeare's drama

[1] As in *Richard III*, where the sleeping power of the army is watched over. Again in *Henry V* the same idea is suggested by the choruses.

[2] See Galsworthy's *Strife* for a modern example of a group action.

we sometimes find a play which appears to be outside this dramatic law, and yet, while it presents the critic with a problem, satisfies his dramatic sense. Such a play is *King Lear*. The play is one in which the idea of poetic justice, which seems to belong to the drama of the individual life, is subordinated, not as in the Greek drama, to the history of a family, but to the issues which control the whole of human life. Where, as in this play, the whole dramatic issues fail to be concentrated in an individual or group consciousness, a reason is given in the structure of the play for this consciousness being in abeyance. Lear's madness, Hamlet's apparent and Ophelia's real derangement, are the ways in which in the plays of *King Lear* and *Hamlet* Shakespeare accounts for the lack of a consistent consciousness of the real issues in the mind of the hero. The irregular movement of the dramatic action in *Hamlet* thus becomes intelligible,[1] and the fateful events in *Lear* are partly brought about by acts of a deranged consciousness. In each case the victim of the conflict is seeking in an unreal world the solution denied to the waking consciousness, and the continuity of the struggle is broken.[2] Some explanation of this kind appears to justify the form of the plays. In Racine's *Phèdre* we have a case in which unconscious impulses almost but not quite overwhelm the action of Phèdre herself; but there is no dislocation of the form of the play.

The admission of this element as a factor in tragedy gives a new method of dramatic values. Every play attempts to represent life through a medium of sym-

[1] The want of form in the play, and of " liaison " between the parts of Victor Hugo's *Hernani* and other plays is a consequence of deficient will-power in the conception of the hero's character.

[2] The same effect is produced by the sleep-walking scene in *Macbeth*.

bolic presentation ; the stage is not the world, but stands for it ; the actors are not humanity, but they play the part. The stage does not merely represent or exaggerate commonplace facts, but aims at producing a picture of life that will have a large appeal.[1] Thus the writer of a play chooses a central element of interest and relates all the surrounding elements to it in a way to produce the necessary effect. Everything depends, as in pictorial art, on the relation between tones and colour, light and shade, in the central and subsidiary actions. There are many methods by which a main element can be made dramatically effective. Corneille in his tragedies gathered together lesser illustrations of the conflict he described and set his central action within them. Racine took a similar plot, isolated the tragic conflict, and concentrated the attention on the central characters. Shakespeare made great use of scenes, humorous or farcical, to illustrate the many different planes of reality within which his tragedy was set. But the one common element in all great tragedies is the reduction to the utmost simplicity of the issues in the great crises and of the words in which these are expressed. The plays of Shakespeare and the drama of Racine both skilfully suggest the atmosphere in which these simple expressions acquire the greatest significance.

There is another reason for the studies of the disintegration of personality that we find in the tragic drama of Racine, and a suggestion of which appears in all great drama. Racine conceived of tragedy as

---

[1] T defect of over-realistic treatment is that we have no guide to the author's view of what is the essential point of interest, because other elements are reproduced without being subordinated. On the other hand, the play with a purpose over-subordinates the other elements of life.

6

illustrating the attack upon and destruction of the individual as the result of an infringement of a social law.   This social law was the moral code of a cultivated society.   The Elizabethan drama, and that of Lope de Vega which was almost contemporary with it, appealed to a large and mixed audience, with which the code was a more primitive one.   Greek drama acknowledged a still more early type of law, involving a family or part of the race in a restricted area ; but as the performance of the tragedy was a national and religious act, the play was in conscious relation to what was understood as the will of the gods, themselves representing natural forces.   Thus the Greek play ultimately acknowledged natural law as interpreted by the religious practice of the nation, Shakespeare's the justice of a mixed society which had a reverence for Divine law, and Racine's was sensitive to the cultivated human social intelligence, to which the ways of God were mysterious, and in which the issue of the moral conflict was in doubt.   In every case dramatic unity is attained, whether the consciousness of the hero is shared or restricted, triumphant or overwhelmed, whether the conflict covers the field of human life or is mainly concerned with an individual, whether the issues can be understood in the light of purely human experience or depend for their interpretation on a belief in a spiritual world.

In the great French neo-classical drama, as also in the preceding Elizabethan drama and the Spanish drama contemporary with both these developments, it is evident that though a theory of form in a play had imposed itself on all who read the current versions of Aristotle's *Poetics*, or the commentaries which found their way into Northern Europe through Italy,[1] the

[1] See Giraldi Cinthio, *Discourse on Comedy and Tragedy*, the views of Castelvetro, and the letters of Scaliger.

great dramatists constructed their plots with knowledge of the unities, but with no slavish adherence to
what was after all a mistaken reading of Aristotle,
whose allusion to a fact of experience in stage-setting
had been erected into a law. Shakespeare openly
put theories aside : Corneille discovered the common
error, and saw that a unity of action was the only
necessity in a play. So he pleaded [1] for a " lieu
théâtral," which is not the same thing as a unity of
place, but an empty stage in which the audience may
see a complicated action carried through without too
greatly disturbing probability. And the more close
the conflict of mind, as in Racine's plays, the less is
the artist troubled by externals in its production, for
the whole interest is absorbed in human interest, and
the probability is a psychological one. The same
reasoning applies to comedy, in which the audience
is hardly conscious of the stage setting unless at any
point in the play it becomes necessary to use the stage
for a crowd, or for comic relief, or for musical interludes.[2] Each of the great dramatists had, explicitly
or implicitly, his own theory of art and of the creation
of illusion on the stage : [3] and a theory which explains
but does not control the form of the play has usually
been evolved at a later date than the play to which
reference has been made.[4]

[1] Corneille, *Discours des Trois Unités.*

[2] Even the comic relief of the interludes serves to carry
on the main interest of the play, as by producing secondary
matter it prevents the onlooker from constructing his own
theory of the plot.

[3] Note, for example, Molière's device for making a play
seem real when in *L'Impromptu de Versailles* he uses the
actual names of his own troupe for the characters, or when,
as in *La Critique de l'Ecole des Femmes,* he makes one of the
characters suggest that their conversation would make a good
play.

[4] This was noticeable in Corneille's *Examens* of his plays.

In the neo-classic period the types of drama are numerous. Tragedy in the seventeenth century ended with the crisis. If the plot were loosely put together, and contained other elements of interest besides the conflict, the play was called a tragi-comedy. Comedy in the neo-classic period might be heroic, like *Le Cid*, or a comedy of manners like the main part of Molière's work, or a " comédie-ballet " including musical interludes. But in general tragedy described events of heroic proportion as a setting to characters of a heroic type, while comedy aimed at a picture of life as experienced, or at any rate as recognized to be true, by the onlookers.

During the first half of the seventeenth century when the way was being prepared in France for the great plays of the later half of the century, and when the art of stage-setting was developing from the simple stage of Corneille to one having elaborate scenes and "machines" which were to constitute one of the attractions of the opera, England was producing masques for which Inigo Jones designed the scenery.[1] With his experience of the Italian stage he used Italian methods and displaced the rougher staging of the sixteenth-century masque. Instead of dispersing properties and scenery he concentrated them and used a painted curtain as a drop-scene. He kept the blue-sky canopy of the Elizabethan masque, but used the Italian perspective construction.[2] His method developed to include the opening of one scene behind another, and " motions " or directions given to different parts of

[1] Sketches of Inigo Jones's plans have been preserved in All Souls' and Christ Church libraries (Oxford) and in the library at Chatsworth. The latter contains sketches dating from 1605–1640. See Enid Welsford, *Italian Influence on the English Court Masque*, Modern Language Review, Oct. 1923.
[2] As in *The Masque of Blackness*, 1605.

the stage. Music was introduced to claim the attention of the audience while a scene was being staged. In every way variety was aimed at. The plan of heading flat scenery by sky pieces was also introduced by Inigo Jones.

It appears, however, that movable scenery (as distinct from flat scenes opening one upon another) was first used for plays at Oxford and Cambridge : though the background of both court masques and University plays was the Vitruvian stage.

The first Stuart kings arranged that adapted pastorals from the French or Italian should be played before the court,[1] with much attention to elaborate costume and staging. The increased interest in spectacular effect on the stage, both in England and on the Continent after 1630, is due to the popularity of the pastoral and to the new " genre " of " tragédie-opera " in which Corneille and Quinault in France became interested, and which furnished in the succeeding century the opportunity for re-telling classical story in a new form.

It should be noticed that in France there was a dual development during this period. The simplicity of the setting of plays by Corneille, Molière, and Racine was suitable because the interest of the audience was altogether concentrated on the action. On the other hand, certain of Corneille's early comedies (in particular *Clitandre*) were full of adventure and change of scene, and resembled a staged romance. Such plays demanded illusion on the stage and created a taste for spectacle. When Richelieu built his great theatre he had *Mirame* performed,[2] a play which could only

[1] E.g. *Florimène*. " The pastorall is in French, and 'tis the argument only, put into English, that I have allowed to be printed."—Adams, *Dramatic Records of Sir Henry Herbert*, p.41.

[2] In 1640.

compel attention by the spectacle which accompanied
it. These two influences, the taste for classic drama
simply produced and the taste for spectacular drama,
affected England both before and after the Restoration. We have already discussed the influence of
French strict theoiy on the later seventeenth-century
stage in England ; it will now be convenient to examine
foreign influences on the English opera and spectacular
drama.

The beginnings of opera on the English stage are
referred to by Dryden in *Of Heroic Plays* as if this
" genre " was a species of entertainment allowed during
the Puritan Revolution, when tragedies and comedies
were alike banned. He refers to the debt the English
producers owed to Italian opera and also to the heroic
drama of the seventeenth century in France. Sir
William D'Avenant, who obtained leave for an operatic
representation in 1656, had however been interested
in a plan for the production of opera from a much earlier
date. The interest of his experiments is briefly that
they emphasized the decorative character of the
setting. The scenes or views were meant to be attrac-
tive and suitable in themselves, but were not necessarily the appropriate setting for the action to be
performed. Here we trace the result of the neo-classical theatre on Vitruvian lines, which was decorative,
and which imposed itself as an ideal on the setting
of seventeenth-century plays. The simpler require-
ments of a neutral space for action, and magnificence
in costume and appointments, which we found were
characteristic of the Elizabethan stage, are lost when
the operatic form is employed. The needs of opera
obliged the producer to have a large stage: Sir William
D'Avenant, in the prefatory address " to the Reader "
in *The Siege of Rhodes*, complains that a stage eleven
feet high and fifteen deep was too narrow for his

programme.[1] Designs by Inigo Jones and John Webb show the elaborate stage suited for operatic "entertainments," which after the Restoration was used for Restoration drama. It had considerable depth, and several types of movable scenery at the back of the stage; side scenes which were far apart in front, and gradually converged, and very elaborate decoration of the proscenium opening.[2]

In 1660 two companies of players, with rights to erect buildings and use music and decoration, were constituted by Charles II. Palladio's *First Book of Architecture* was translated in 1663, and was followed by a renewed interest in the architecture of the stage. Sir Christopher Wren designed the theatre in Dorset Garden, and the king's players went to a new theatre and opera house at Drury Lane. In course of time the companies coalesced, and the stage of Drury Lane was remodelled in 1693 : boxes were added, and new stage doors were placed in the proscenium.

[1] For this and many other details I am indebted to L. B. Campbell, *Scenes and Machines on the English Stage*, Part IV.

[2] We trace here the origins of the " picture " stage of modern times, in which the action is framed by the stage opening, and there is no Elizabethan " apron." The analogy is with the Vitruvian theatre and the French classical stage rather than with mediæval stage practice.

CHAPTER V

THE MODERN PERIOD

(a) Influence of Neo-classicism in the second part of the Seventeenth Century and in the Eighteenth Century

IN France the great neo-classical period had been prepared for by Hardy's experiments in tragi-comedy and Garnier's and Rotrou's adaptation of Greek plots, and in the seventeenth century its progress was uninterrupted. But England in the seventeenth century was suffering under the blight caused by the Civil War and the Puritan Revolution. Thus in England dramatic production was officially cut short in the year 1642, and only a few clownish plays, which were not produced at regular theatres, kept alive the popular interest in drama, while spectacle was produced at irregular intervals for the entertainment of the cultivated classes.

When, in 1660, the Restoration took place and the ban on the drama was removed, the consistent tradition of the theatre in England had been broken and was not without difficulty partially recovered, though the tradition of stage structure had persisted. Unquestionably, too, the theatre after 1660 became not so much the expression of national life (as it had been in the Elizabethan period), as the expression of one section of society, aristocratic, but to a large extent inefficient in politics and unsatisfactory in its moral outlook. To an enthusiasm for national life, to the spirit of adventure, to a deep sense of the final issues of good and bad conduct, had succeeded disillusionment and a recoil to reason from sentiment. These influences produced a satirical view of life, and the rise of a scientific spirit at the same epoch [1] tended to make the literature of the period realistic. In fact, while France was reducing a very vivid and full life to rule in her classical period, England was basing both her dramatic theory and practice on the experience of France, and contributing little herself to dramatic expression. It was not until 1688 that an equilibrium in society was reached in England which helped literature to develop in more individual and characteristic channels. The establishment of the principles of civil and religious liberty then made possible the creation of new forms of national literature.

The drama in England between 1660 and 1688 was chiefly derived from French models. The setting of these plays, though transferred to an English atmosphere by the use of English personal and place names, was in reality romantic in the sense of being remote from actual experience. This remoteness is emphasized by the symbolism used in many of the names: for the adapters recognized that many of the characters in French classical comedy were types as well as individuals and it was the sense of the type or condition of the character that was transmitted to the English stage. We may instance such names as Sir Positive At-All, in Shadwell's *The Sullen Lovers* (built upon Molière's *Les Facheux*), Sir Jasper Fidget,

[1] The foundation of the Royal Society, 1663, is a key to the spirit of the period.

and old Lady Squeamish in Wycherley's *The Country Wife* (based upon Molière's *L'Ecole des Maris* and *L'Ecole des Femmes*), as examples of the method by which the framework of the French play was transferred to the English stage, while the realistic detail with which the plays were loaded illustrated English and not French life.

It is due to French influence that the rhymed heroic couplet was used in the dramatic work of D'Avenant and Dryden, and developed by Etheredge and Lord Orrery.   But plays written in heroic couplets had the character of the tragi-comedy, which needs a more grandiloquent setting than pure comedy, and later writers, such as Shadwell and Wycherley, used prose.   A third characteristic of Restoration drama is the free use of prologues and epilogues.   These introductions and " last words " in a play, spoken by the author, repeated by an actor, or contributed by a friend or collaborator or patron, were intended (like the similar additions made to Seneca's tragedies) to claim the interest of the audience by a personal appeal, or to set forth a theory of drama of which the play is the illustration, or, as in Plautus' comedies, to complete the unwinding of the meshes of the plot.[1]   In every case they divert attention from the dramatic value of the play as such, and are perhaps a warning that instead of working on the theory " the play's the thing," the dramatists of the Restoration had to chaperone their handiwork on its first appearance in public.   The personal allusions, both political and social, permitted in a prologue or epilogue,

---

[1] Lessing, *Hamburgische Dramaturgie* (erste Band, Siebentes Stück), gives an account of the English addiction to prologues and epilogues, and the utility of these in securing appreciation for a new piece.   They began to be important in the plays of Shakespeare's immediate successors.

often added the element of a " succès de scandale." [1]

In plays of this character the monologue was an important feature. At first the monologues were imitated from those in the plays of Corneille, which were used as models, and were thus narrative or descriptive, but in a later writer, Congreve, they were employed as opportunities for unmasking a villain to the audience, and as such they have the psychological importance of the monologues in Racine. They occur in plays in which the events are sufficiently far-fetched to be remote from the actual experience of the lookers-on, and the monologue is a means of drawing audience and characters together in a closer relation, otherwise denied to a Restoration audience and the " persons of quality " on the stage.

Two other points should be noticed in connexion with English Restoration drama. The experiments of Sir John Vanbrugh in stage-setting at the end of his life illustrate a weak point in structure. It was the desire of Vanbrugh and of his contemporaries to produce splendid and decorative buildings which had little practical value for the production of a play. In this they reproduced the conception of the late Roman and early Italian theatres, which were more suited for recitation than for action, and transmitted a side of the foreign classical spirit which was not suited to the England of their day.

The other point is the confusion made by contemporary critics, the most important of whom was Jeremy Collier, between the art of the stage and the life which it reflected. Here it is the didactic side of the foreign neo-classic play which has overwhelmed English

---

[1] Shadwell, in *The Sullen Lovers*, Act I, sc. 2, alludes to the flourish of trumpets with which the entrance of witches in a play is emphasized. Here again the incidents have to be artificially supported.

thinkers.   The coarseness of drama can only be cured by refining life and not by eliminating from drama its significance as a reflection of the contemporary national spirit.

Neo-classicism in the drama was in fact a form of the logical or rational spirit.   This shows itself in two ways : first in an effort to make plots consecutive and likely, and to lead to an inevitable *dénouement*, and secondly (and this often occurs in later experiments) in an effort to make the drama a vehicle of didactic teaching.   In France the order was reversed : Corneille's work was didactic and Racine's plots were more consistent.   In Spain, where the interest was at first mainly in the neo-classic method, rather than in the moral issues of the drama, the course of development differs from that in France.   A contributory cause was the fact that Spain was affected by French influence of the period of Racine through the court of Philip V of Spain (the grandson of Louis XIV).   After 1710, when the king felt secure on his throne, festivities at court began to be organized : and among the first entertainments was the performance of a play by Corneille : while in 1713 a Royal Academy of a French pattern was established in Spain.   We find contemporary authors explaining that the grand manner of Corneille was more suitable to the court than the native Spanish plays in which great freedom of speech was allowed, and which had " ni règles ni décence."   After the death of Marie of Savoy till the king's death in 1746, there was very little done in the way of entertainment by the court.   The influence on Spain after about 1714 was a more direct literary one.[1]

[1] According to Feijóo (*Teatro Critico*) the habit of Gongorism or preciosity was gaining on Spain because of the difficulty of distinguishing between "elevated style and affectation."   Feijóo criticized the Spaniards who rejected

The task of re-introducing the Aristotelean rules into Spanish drama was undertaken by Luzán, who was aware of them through his Italian studies.[1] His view was that the force of Spanish genius needed the restraining curb which would enable it to show itself in perfect form. While, however, the more forcible is French genius, the more it regards form, Spanish literature, like English, is more instinctive, less conscious of its own force and less able to apply the curb.[2]

Luzán, following the neo-classics, emphasized the necessity of a moral purpose in drama. It is curious to see how every critic who cares about form in art, from Boileau to Bergson, finds himself obliged to work in this direction. The subject was kept alive in Spain by the publication from 1723 onwards of a regular *critique* on contemporary work. The object of the editors was to repress typically Spanish vices, such as exaggeration and scenes of violence, but the correction was violently administered and failed in its effect.

In 1749 the effort to strengthen the neo-classic spirit was begun by a number of academies, which

French influence, and also those who allowed their national feeling to be overwhelmed. He considered classic work to be the result of clarifying and reducing thoughts to form, but he also gave a value to uncriticized impressions, the "je ne sais quoi" which is unused and formless material. See Pellissier, *The Neo-Classic Movement in Spain during the Eighteenth Century*, and L. P. Thomas, *Le Lyrisme et la Préciosité cultistes en Espagne*, Paris, 1909.

[1] Luzán, *Poetica*.

[2] Luzán, however, avoided certain difficulties of the theorist by showing that the artist, in imitating nature, could imitate a general and ideal character of nature and also individual and concrete examples of life. He showed, too, that imagination could be said to be true to fact if the conditions from which it arises were admitted to be true. There is, then, a rationalized imagination. Cf. Bergson, *Le Rire*.

from their origin had the character of the French *salon*,
and inculcated the courtesy of the *précieux* school,
together with the feeling for simplicity of the early
romantics. The critics who did their early work in
these *salons* were anxious to find examples of regular
plays in Spanish, but the only one that fulfilled the
somewhat severe test of the neo-classic was *La Elisa
Dido* by Virtués. Montiano's *Virginia*, written without knowledge of Campistron's play, is also regular,
and is, as the author assures us, an illustration of a
complete heroic action. By the end of the eighteenth
century we have regular comedies, such as Yriarte's
El Señorito Mimado.

It was, however, noticed by contemporary observers
that the architecture of the Spanish stage at this
period kept its traditional form, and that it was not
till 1740 that a large theatre modelled on the Italian
type was built at Madrid. The Spanish theatre of
the eighteenth century was square or oblong, retaining
the shape of the " patio " or court-yard. A very
elaborate system of seating, by which men and women
were accommodated in different parts of the theatre,
and the civil magistrates had boxes assigned to their
use, prevailed in Spain. The " parterre," or pit, retained the name of " patio." Benches were placed
to the right and left of the stage, a custom that prevailed in France up to Voltaire's middle period. The
Spanish theatre had rows of boxes on the first floor
of the building and a second row for people who
wished to see without being observed. Riccoboni [1]
notices the extreme simplicity of the staging and
scenery up to the middle of the eighteenth century,
when the advent of opera brought with it a taste
for luxury. But he also notices that the natural and
vivid gesture of the Spanish actor rendered him inde-

[1] *Réflexions sur les Théâtres*, etc.

pendent of costume and accessories.[1] This was especially the case with the " gracioso," the person who played the chief part in the comedies.

Drama is, as has been said, the literature of those who do not read. There were two audiences from the sixteenth century onwards in the three Latin countries, Spain, Italy, France : the people to whom the drama was the reality of romance, and the learned society to which it represented also a literary tradition. We have seen that while the audiences in the sixteenth century were mixed, they tended in France to become purely literary in the seventeenth. The recovery of the classic tradition was the result in France : Italy retained her popular comedy in full force till the eighteenth century, Spain had her national theatre in the sixteenth and seventeenth centuries. In the eighteenth century, however, new developments occur in all three countries.

In Spain we have the least fortunate result, for the springs of national inspiration had run dry, and imitations of French classical plays were weaker in their translated form. We have seen, too, that in Spain in the seventeenth and eighteenth centuries theory preceded practice. But Italy produced in the eighteenth century a new comedy according to the rules, with Goldoni : and France made a series of experiments in *bourgeois* comedy, *drame larmoyant*, and romantic historical plays. Both in France and

[1] *Op. cit.*, p. 62, " . . . ayant rencontré un jour un Comédien Espagnol, je le priai de me réciter quelques scènes : il le fit d'une façon qui me surprit, et me pénétra tellement que je ne l'ai jamais oublié : j'en fus d'autant plus surpris, que son habit ne lui étoit point avantageux pour déclamer quelque chose de noble : car, il n'avoit pour tout équipage qu'une sonquenille de toile noire, avec laquelle il allait en pélérinage à Rome."

Italy one great change took place. The actors aimed,
not at a romantic remoteness, but at a realistic acces-
sibility—their effort was to become one with the audience and please by contact and familiarity.

The stages in both countries acquired scenery of a
realistic kind. Mercier and Diderot give directions
for this with the conscientiousness of Ibsen at a later
epoch. The climax was said to have been reached in
Paris when a young man in the audience, struck with
pity for the poverty of a character on the stage, ran up
and offered her his purse. This absent-minded gener-
osity was regarded as a proof of realism of presentation and also of the fulfilment of a function of the
drama, which was then understood to be the awaken-
ing of sensibility in the audience.

Goldoni in Italy produced a similar change. He
dispensed with the typical characters of the masque,
and also with the witty heroines, one of whom, the
famous Silvia, became the inspiration of Marivaux
in France. The landlady, the shop-girl, the lodger,
the peasant, all in their appropriate and present-day
clothes, move across his stage, their language is that
heard in the street and in the piazza : the action has
the peculiarly rapid Italian quality : everything is
sufficiently enhanced to be interesting, sufficiently
real to be familiar. Like Diderot he adds the special
touches that betray a man's occupation as well as
his character.

For a play of this kind, whether in France or Italy,
indoor scenes became necessary and frequent changes
of scene desirable. It is true that the convention
of a neutral place was occasionally kept. In France
this tended to be the antechamber, and on one occasion the author advised that in the wait between scenes
servants should move backwards and forwards to
keep up the illusion that life was going on even when

not openly represented there.[1] The rooms and properties, too, were commendably simple. Furniture would have been in the way of the stirring Italian actors. At the same time scenery showed the local differences between one street and another, one house and another.

Goldoni's comedy has a quality which is rare, but curiously interesting. In Molière's comedies there is always one character—generally the servant—who can see and comment with cool common sense on the absurdities of the chief actors. We have therefore every plane of comedy represented and the relation of these planes defined. But in Goldoni there is no such detached character who comments on the rest. Any Italian character in comedy turns upon himself and laughs at his own mistakes as well as at those of others. Every one is perpetually becoming conscious of himself and therefore also humorous.

Goldoni accepted the traditional division of a play into three acts and rather arbitrarily schemed his plays accordingly. As we have seen, he changed quickly from a scene within to one without the house. New methods of lighting the stage in the eighteenth century made it possible for a character to retire into the background and yet be visible to the audience. Hence the new importance of by-play : it becomes part of a composition that has depth as well as width.

The history of stage-production in the Netherlands was largely affected by the history of the people. Subject to great political changes, which prevented a steady development of the arts, the Low Countries possessed a relatively rough folk-drama, presented by different corporations as " Kamerspel," when played indoors, or as " Parades " on rough boards at the village fairs or Kermesses ; but from time to time foreign influences controlled the fashion of any

[1] Beaumarchais, *Eugénie*.

7

more cultivated drama in the country. National taste dictated an extreme realism in the presentation of all plays : the tragedy-of-blood in Holland was spectacular and exaggerated. Sensational effects were desired and obtained. The action too was interrupted by tableaux containing a large number of actors grouped in position to represent some scene which was a key to the meaning of the play. These tableaux were inserted awkwardly, often in the middle of an act.

But the influence of the French classical drama gradually drove out over-emphasis, and the eighteenth century saw plays of regular form written in Alexandrines.

The shape of a Dutch theatre (as at Amsterdam and The Hague) was semi-circular, or rather semi-oval : the stage touching the diameter. The parterre was seated, and steps beyond it led to standing room. Boxes were placed on the first-floor level round the auditorium. The shape resembled the Vitruvian model, while the arrangement was Spanish. The early eighteenth century was the time in which the Dutch theatre was most productive, but its earlier folk-comedies affected Germany.

The relation between the drama and the art of stage-production is less close in Germany than in the countries of the Latin peoples, or than in England. There are several reasons for this distinction. The drama of the Middle Ages and period of the Renaissance in Europe was produced under the influence of the courts, the universities and schools, and gradually became a drama which had a popular and national appeal. But in Germany, broken up into provinces with separate political interests, and after the Reformation with separate religious aims, there was no national or popular tribunal to which to appeal, neither were there universities to transmit the influence of classical models, and to encourage new inventions, till the period of the Renaissance. And this new life was cut short by the Thirty Years War, which drained German intellectual and artistic life of its force, and made a new revival in letters necessary in the eighteenth century.[1]

There was a second reason for a delay before German dramatic work was ready to count as a factor in European literary activity. The drama is pre-eminently a social art : it is a stimulus to society or a criticism of it. But the tendency of the German mind is to individual rather than social expression. Hence many German plays were written to give effect to the author's views, and many more without the imaginative realization of what could or could not be successfully produced on a stage. Thus, even in the time of her great dramatists, Goethe and Schiller, plays were produced for the court theatres, and appealed to a very restricted section of the people in some one province in Germany. Goethe had full authority in the production of plays in the court theatre at Weimar, but no wide stimulus from the audience for which these plays were performed.

The first attempt at a general appeal was made

---

[1] We can, however, trace in the life of the German town elements which tended to a development of popular drama. The plays of Hans Sachs, in the latter part of the sixteenth century, are dialogues set in a simple frame, their form defined by the Ehrenhold, or herald. The herald speaks the prologue and epilogue and occasionally guides the action. There is a strong resemblance between his manner and that of the English folk-player of the fifteenth century. In both cases there is a familiar treatment of the Divine persons in a story which brings it within the comprehension of the simple mind. Except for the presence of the herald it could hardly be said to be staged.

in Germany by strolling players who had come from the different universities (especially from the Netherlands) and adapted the plays they had seen and known there to the taste of a popular group. At the end of the sixteenth century these men were known as the " English Actors," and they gave adaptations of Shakespeare's plays. Later, other similar groups introduced plays with Greek plots, and versions of Corneille, Molière, and Racine. A farcical element was inserted into the tragedies to please the people. An attempt was made by Jakob Ayrer to combine the method of the English players with subject-matter similar to that of Hans Sachs, but greatly extended. In Ayrer's plays the clown, instead of filling up the intervals of dialogue, is an actor. Ayrer, too, connects several plays to form a cycle, thus making a double impression on the audience, which recognizes some characters as familiar friends and accepts others as new.

In the seventeenth century Andreas Gryphius carried on the tradition of the English Actors, but though he showed traces of an interest in the supernatural and in the development of a violent central action,[1] his technique was deficient, and there was no opportunity for the emergence of a more characteristic national drama till Gottsched attempted to recreate in Germany the art of staging plays. This he did chiefly by arranging for the performance of tragedies and comedies, translated or adapted from French, English, or Danish.[2]

---

[1] In this he felt the influence of Seneca, who shared with Sophocles the position of classical tragedian. See P. Stachel, *Seneca und das Deutsche Renaissance Drama*, ch. 4.

[2] Home-grown Danish plays, with simple plots and numerous characters, alternated in the Danish theatre with classical plays.

Gradually, however, the introduction of the " comédie bourgeoise " of the eighteenth century into Germany resulted in a home-grown domestic drama, of which Lessing's plays are the most important examples. Like the French eighteenth-century dramatists, Lessing drew both plot and characters and sentiment from English domestic drama and the English novel. Lillo's *London Merchant* (1731) and Richardson's *Clarissa Harlowe* (1748) both affected *Miss Sara Sampson*, written in 1755, which preceded Diderot's *Le fils naturel* by two years.

CHAPTER VI

THE MODERN PERIOD

(b) New Theories of Drama and Staging in the Eighteenth Century

A STRIKING characteristic of all French dramtic work from the sixteenth century onwards had been its expression of a consciously conceived social idea. The figures in French drama are alive at every point to their relations with one another, and the morality implied is that of a well-ordered society. It was a shock to French feeling when Racine put upon the stage a figure like his Phèdre, moved by blind hereditary impulse. The criticism of Port Royal was here at one with that of French society as a whole: it was generally felt that the picture of manners was below the ideal standard of modern life, and that primitive and uncontrolled passion should not be exhibited on the stage.[1] And yet there existed similar material for the painting of emotion in Greek and English plays: Sophocles, Euripides, and Shakespeare in depicting life had suggested the existence of an undercurrent out of

---

[1] It is true that the Jansenists after closer examination agreed that *Phèdre* was not a bad play, for it showed the terrible consequence of primitive hereditary passion in a morbid and undisciplined life.

which the acts and the facts of visible experience emerge. In all these writers the force of national and family life supplied a background to individual emotion, and was itself subject to higher powers. French art as a rule suggested the existence of this latent force in the crowd, the people or army, where also it is rapidly communicated and gains strength by cohesion, but the French, in their studies of the individual life, drew little attention to the dramatic value of impulse until their attention was gradually diverted from the classical idea of the conflict of the will to the analysis of emotion which we find in eighteenth-century literature. The eighteenth century, then, is a time of transition, and the somewhat blind experiments in *drame* and in tragedy during that period have the interest to the psychologist of preparing the way for a wider conception of drama, one in which the life of the present is seen linked to that of the past : in which individual impulses are revealed against a background of racial and social experience.[1]

In developing the history of the tragic idea in French drama from the seventeenth to the nineteenth century we have to deal with two main currents of influence. First there was the influence of Racine, which insensibly affected the painting of the subconscious mind in later writers, and opened the way to the psychological drama, in which, whatever are the main events, the interest is concentrated on the struggle within the minds of the chief characters. Secondly, when this influence was on the wane, the translations of Shakespeare's tragedies and the return-

[1] See Guiraud in the *Muse Française*, t. 2, p. 21 (1824) : "Mais lorsque les évènemens font rentrer la vie dans le cœur, lorsque la patrie, la famille, le moi, sont ménacés, tous les sentimens énergiques se reveillent."

ing interest in Greek drama drew the attention of France to the portrayal of conflict in other forms than that of French seventeenth-century tragedy. Critics were obliged to acknowledge that the type of play thus presented to them was a true one, though not a " genre " hitherto known in France. Thus a new theory of the drama became possible at the end of the eighteenth century, in which all the experiments then made could find their place.

Tragedy holds more closely to tradition than comedy; and the immediate successors of Corneille and Racine did little to modify the classical method. But the over-emphatic school of Crébillon embarrassed the stage with a very complicated intrigue ; and the horrors that he piled up diminished the sense of reality felt by the audience. The over-rhetorical plays of Voltaire would have had exactly the same result, if he had not learned during his visit to England something of the spectacular effect which is produced in an Elizabethan play by the participation of the crowd in the action. It is due to Voltaire that the spectators were finally removed from the narrow French stage, and room given for larger numbers of minor characters to act in groups. Voltaire saw, too, that attempts at realistic decoration and scenery would fail so long as the spectators were too near to the action.[1] In the early play of *Œdipe*, Voltaire had already perceived that the threatening cries of the people, even though no one appeared on the stage, would produce a tragic atmosphere. He said in the preface to *Semiramis* (1748) that the sense of declamation and the desire for a spectacle on the stage, both of which were satisfied by " tragédie-opéra " were a nearer approach to the Greek emotional spirit shown in rhythm than the method of one of the ordinary classical representations,

[1] *Discours sur la tragédie.*

and he could refer to contemporary " tragédie-opéra " for the proof of his views.

Voltaire and M. J. Chénier, though by very different methods, produced a unity in their tragic drama. Voltaire, in the Roman plays, depicts characters which are all moved by a love of country that takes the place of the motive supplied by the laws of honour in Spanish drama, or the sense of destiny in the Greek and in the French classic drama. Chénier has a strong conception of the unity of the race in time. This is especially shown in *Charles IX* and in *Tibère*. A tragedy in his hands is both historical and applicable to present conditions ; and it refers to the influence of the unseen life of the past on the present and on the future. Such plays demand a certain symbolic presentation and the idea of France and of Rome is suggested by typical groups of people. An over-mastering emotional atmosphere is closely connected with this setting of the play.

In another direction, more closely connected with the æsthetic than with the practice of the stage, the eighteenth century marked the transition from seventeenth to nineteenth century ideals. The practical development is illustrated in the arguments used by Sebastian Mercier for a national art of the theatre in France.[1] Though unable to feel the full charm and the dramatic value of history, this critic urged the representation on the stage of contemporary national life and movements. His theory was founded on the belief that art is ultimately for the people : the change from aristocracy to democracy was significant, so Mercier thought, of that from the old drama to the new. For to his mind the tendency of the classical drama was aristocratic : it should make way for *drame*, which reflected the joys and sorrows of ordinary

[1] Mercier, *Du Théâtre.*

men : and which should take the place of the ancient
tragedy.

But Mercier, and also Diderot, had other though
unavowed reasons for neglecting tragedy in their
theory of the drama. They shrank from picturing
the emotion that is produced by conflict. Mercier
through his belief in the prevailing power of goodness,
and Diderot through his habit of blurring moral
distinctions, felt that very little was really at stake
in this world. Thus they produced an accommodation between the world as they conceived it and the
characters with which they peopled their plays. Compromise was the rule of their drama. This was helped
in the case of Mercier by some romantic circumstances
and melodramatic conclusions, and in the case of
Diderot by an occasional vein of satire which enabled
the author to put his play into perspective or judge
the characters from a single point of view. Both
Mercier and Diderot had a sense of dramatic unity,
and to that sense they really sacrificed their other
principles. The other principles they had adopted
from the contemporary philosophy of the eighteenth
century, namely those of moral utility and of realism,
are not only incompatible with one another, but
they are external to the notion of the conflict of the
will which is essential to many types of drama.

Certain experiments in comedy, those of Marivaux,
Le Sage, and Beaumarchais, relieved the prevailing
sentimental atmosphere of the eighteenth century in
France. Marivaux admitted fanciful elements from
the Italian harlequinade into his comedy of social life,
and as he humanized Harlequin and placed all his
characters in a charming, if at times artificial setting,
the plays had their own character in which Marivaux
had an opportunity for working out a psychology of
the emotions.

Le Sage produced a vigorous satire on a society that was working up to a revolution. He obtained his effects by realism, but showed everything moving at a quicker pace on the stage than in life. Beaumarchais had a more definite theory of drama than his predecessors. He had a dominant character in Figaro, who pointed the meaning of the play. Beaumarchais, except in his last play, deliberately avoided the method of *drame*, but left careful stage directions for the use of telling costumes and accessories. As against writers of *drame*, writers of comedy kept up the traditional view that the stage should contain a neutral space in which the main action of the play was staged.

The theatres of the eighteenth century in France had begun to use more elaborate stage scenery, following the example of the opera. This scenery in the case of *drame* was as realistic and life-like as possible [1] and this plan was in accordance with the dramatic theory of the time, which had decided that the stage should be an expression of contemporary national life.

At the end of the eighteenth century the settings of comedy and *drame* were purely realistic, but that of tragedy was symbolic, and a large number of allegorical plays and pageants were produced.

In Germany the advance made by Lessing was chiefly in the domain of criticism. In his plays, formed on the pattern of the " drame bourgeois," we see the eighteenth-century characteristics with little new matter added. [2] But Germany owes to Lessing the inauguration of a national dramatic spirit, and

---

[1] For example, in staging plays by Nivelle de la Chaussée, Voltaire's plays of sentiment, and the plays of Diderot and Mercier.

[2] Cf. *Minna von Barnhelm.*

a deliberate attempt to recover natural and simple lines of structure for the play in opposition to the artificiality which invaded German versions of French neo-classical plays.

The most important period of German dramatic literature after its inauguration by Lessing in 1764, lies between 1771 and 1805, and covers the time of Goethe's and Schiller's best dramatic work.

It should be noticed, however, that the advent of a great dramatic literature in Germany at the end of the eighteenth century corresponds more closely both in time and in the spirit of the work to the French historical drama of the end of the eighteenth century than to a Romantic literature properly so called. Germany was influenced (as Madame de Staël has pointed out) in a deeper and more lasting way by J. J. Rousseau than were other countries of Europe. The emotion disengaged by the stimulus administered by Rousseau found its way out in the " Sturm und Drang " movement, and the plays written by Goethe and Schiller in this period take rank as " classical " plays. For there was a well-defined intention on the part of these authors to write with a large conception of life which they owed to their classical studies, and to add to this the material gained in the more recent history of their nation. They also took an interest in other national developments of art, particularly in that of Shakespeare in England. Thus, in the hands of Goethe, while his drama tended to expand emotion, his study of the classics of Greece and Rome produced both a method and a series of subjects for treatment. His strong and varied genius attempted many forms of dramatic expression to which he gave a national application.[1]

[1] After his Italian journey the classical influence predominated in his thought.

So far as the new spirit in Germany drew its strength from its opposition to the rationalizing spirit of the eighteenth century, so far its writers turned for inspiration to Shakespeare, who dominated dramatic conceptions in Germany before 1824 [1] and in France chiefly after that date.[2] It is characteristic of a literary revolt to look into the history of the past for new models. Thus the Middle Ages, with their superstitious terrors, the Elizabethan period with its fresh adventurousness, became real to the German writer, who expressed in literary form the aspirations of the nation and the individual. Among the debts of the German drama of the classical period to Shakespeare should be mentioned the inclusion of songs in a play. Not only the comedies, but the tragedies of Shakespeare have these song interludes: *A Midsummer Night's Dream*, *As You Like It*, and *Hamlet* all contributed to suggest this method of emotional relief to the German dramatist.[3]

Songs occur in Goethe's *Götz von Berlichingen* (Acts II and III), Clärchen sings in *Egmont* (Act III): even in a metrical play, such as *Iphigenie*, there is

[1] See A. W. Schlegel's translation of Shakespeare, 1797.

[2] See, however, French translations and adaptations of Shakespeare by Le Tourneur and Ducis which affected French taste before 1789.

[3] The subject of the dramatic value of the songs in Shakespeare has been recently treated by Richmond Noble (*Shakespeare's Use of Song*, 1923). It appears that the introduction of songs in the early plays was external to the plot and characters: in *Love's Labour Lost*, 1597, two songs were added to the play which have the same tone as the comedy, but were not an original part of it. With the development of Shakespeare's art, music as introduced into *The Merchant of Venice* and *A Midsummer Night's Dream* has dramatic meaning; and this is even more strongly pressed in the tragedies. In *The Tempest* the relation of the songs to the masque should be noted.

a song in short metre (Act IV) besides a certain variety in the verse. As the dialogue and character-drawing in these plays is assimilated as far as possible to natural experience, the introduction of songs supplies a perspective of expression on the stage. Clärchen, for instance, betrays herself, and Iphigenia becomes the prophetess, when under the influence suggested by the song.

In Schiller's dramas, too, for instance in *Wilhelm Tell*, songs give the play atmosphere and background. It is clear that the German dramatist felt the danger of monotony and tried to overcome it in the Shakespearean manner.

It becomes evident, in a study of the German classical period, that though all the elements of Romanticism, mediæval and picturesque setting and defiance of convention, were there present, the element of preoccupation with the self was perhaps the strongest in German drama. The author identified himself, his personal views and his inner conflict, with the hero of his play; and this gives to the German classical drama a sense of unity that is absent from many contemporary plays in France.

This sense of unity was deliberately developed both by Goethe and Schiller. The period of the friendship of the two poets was especially fruitful in regard to this question—for both Goethe and Schiller wished to produce a new art which should combine the ideals of Greece and the modern world.[1] It is no doubt for this reason that Schiller, in his greatest historical drama, *Wallenstein*, attempted the plan of a trilogy.

---

[1] See, on this point, Goethe's rules for actors. He differs from the usual practice of the stage as he advises the actors never to forget the audience but to attend to the "third person," thus creating a link between the stage and the world.

This was not altogether successful for two reasons: the original conception took the form of a long ten-act play with a prologue, *Wallensteins Lager*, and this is more consistent with Schiller's idea than the later development of three plays. Secondly, the Greek trilogy depended for its interest on the continued attendance of the audience at all three plays. When *Die Piccolomini* is considered separately, it is too clearly only the first part of a tragedy, and is incomplete and not an organic whole. The plays do, however, fulfil the condition, which Aristotle discovered in Greek tragedy, of being " of a certain magnitude," while atmosphere is produced, as in Shakespeare's plays, by the crowd ; in this case by Wallenstein's soldiers. So far Schiller has successfully combined ancient and modern theory.

In certain other plays, as for example in *Die Jungfrau von Orleans* and *Maria Stuart*, he has aimed at unity and at human appeal, but sacrificed historical fact and probability. Such plays were not historic dramas, but stories which owed little but picturesqueness to the historical imagination. *Die Braut von Messina* is a more satisfactory attempt at the reproduction of the classical atmosphere as shown in the fate-motive that directs the movement of the plays. But Schiller's imitation of Greek models has here led him to include a chorus, and the chorus is, strictly speaking, more like those of Seneca than those of the Greek dramatists, and therefore has no particular dramatic significance. In fact the failure of *Die Braut von Messina* as a play to be acted is partly due to this error of construction and partly to the uncertainty of the author about the use of the fate-motive.

The German ideal of dramatic representation is really more akin to that of the German epic or saga, which lends itself to musical or operatic form. The instinct for form and atmosphere of Goethe and Schiller is very similar to that felt by Richard Wagner. All three great artists need an element of unity and of picturesqueness which finds its best illustration in recurring *motifs* and musical rhythm.[1]

England, at the end of the eighteenth century, produced a natural and spontaneous comedy-of-manners in the work of Goldsmith and Sheridan. Although the characters in these plays retained the symbolic names with which Restoration comedy had made English playgoers familiar,[2] the dialogue was easy and realistic, scenes of humour alternated with pathos which appealed to an English audience, and the " ingénue " who had played such an important part in French comedy from the time of Molière, appeared on the English stage.

The scenery of these plays at the London theatres was simple, and mainly represented interiors, as on the French stage of the same period, but the costumes were rich and striking and gave a note of distinction to the presentation. The fashion of the time, both in tragedy (either Shakespearean or derived from foreign sources) and comedy, was for intensity rather than for violence in action, and the age was one of great actors in England, including Mrs. Siddons, the Kembles, and Edmund Kean.

In the London theatres of the end of the eighteenth century, for example in the new Drury Lane and the New Haymarket, the stage was deep from back

[1] See J. C. F. von Schiller, " Perception with me is at first without a clear and definite object ; this forms itself later.   A certain musical mood of mind precedes, and only after this does the poetical idea follow with me."

[2] E.g. Sir Anthony Absolute, Miss Lydia Languish, and Sir Lucius O'Trigger in Sheridan's *The Rivals*, Croaker in Goldsmith's *The Good Natured Man*, Joseph Surface and Sir Peter Teazle in *The School for Scandal*.

to front, and as the scenery was simple and mainly
composed of canvas, the characters who had speaking
parts came forward as far as possible.   Thus exits
and entrances were supplied by large doors to the
right and left of the proscenium.   This arrangement
was peculiar to the English stage of the period.   Chande-
liers hanging from the roof of the proscenium were
used for lighting as well as footlights and lights to
the right and left of the stage.   With the disappear-
ance of the great English actors and actresses of the
eighteenth century, and the increased attention to
spectacular effect, the English stage entered upon a
new and less fruitful period at the beginning of the
nineteenth century.

8

CHAPTER VII

THE MODERN PERIOD

(c) ROMANTICISM

IN France, the immediate effect of the history summarized in periods of the Revolution, the Terror, the Consulate, and the Empire, had been to produce " pièces de circonstance " ; and it is a healthy sign of the vitality of the stage in France that although different " troupes " were organized under the Terror to present a political view to the public, and force it to accept this view at a represen-tation, every change in the political situation was reflected in satiric comedy. In comedy of this species dress was modern, though a foreign or ancient plot might supply the skeleton of the play ; the modern application of the sentiments uttered on the boards was so essential to the understanding of the drama that the dress of an Incroyable, of a Garde nationale, the " carmagnole " and " bonnet rouge " of the Jacobin, were transferred from the street to the stage.

In the years of sudden change that marked the period of the First Empire and the Restoration, plays appeared on the French stage in which political allusions could be adapted to different circumstances. Thus *Le Triomphe de Trajan*, which was intended as homage to Napoleon I, was put on the bill, though owing to the illness of an actor not actually played, in Paris

when the Allies were in occupation. At the time of
the Restoration, plays about Henry IV (*Partie de
Chasse de Henri IV, Souper de Henri IV*, and others)
were greatly in vogue. But these facts prove above
all things the absence of an independent dramatic
spirit. The tragedies played were all traditional, and
the comedies were of the nature of the vaudeville.

From 1815 onwards, however, the increasing stability
of French society showed itself in dramatic work, very
often of a melodramatic order, whether under the
name of tragedy or comedy, which criticized in turn
the Revolution and the Napoleonic wars. The death
of Robespierre had before that time been celebrated
on the stage,[1] and a play of a similar type was Arnault's
Germanicus, acted in 1817 and in 1824. But this
" genre " gave way gradually to light comedy of
the kind represented by Scribe and Dupin.

The real originator of the light satirical comedy,
interspersed at times with music, and written in
prose, instead of, like the light comedy of the last
days of the monarchy, in verse, was L. B. Picard.
Napoleon had a travelling theatre with him in his
campaigns, and the plays represented were those that
afforded the greatest possible contrast to a military
life : namely a description of " les mœurs du province."
In this Picard excelled, and there was a caustic humour
and a sense of disillusionment with heroic ideas—a
reference, too, to the avarice and profiteering of
certain classes of the nation which fitted in well with
the experience of the moment.[2] The *mise-en-scène*
was of the simplest, and pictorial effect was gained

---

[1] In 1795 and 1802.
[2] One of his plays, *La Petite Ville*, was adapted at the end
of the nineteenth century in Germany as *Die Lustige
Wittwe*, and made its appearance in England as *The Merry
Widow*.

by the costume for which Picard was left careful directions. Exits and entrances were arranged to keep the play going without waits or " longueurs." [1]

The effect of this method on the stage of Paris was entirely satisfactory, for the onus of arousing interest was now on the actors and the piece itself, instead of on spectacle as at the opera, or on the political allusions of serious drama. [2]

Scribe's first play was *Le Prétendant par hasard* acted in 1810, and he wrote copiously till about 1851, when Augier's more solid comedy was already in the ascendant, and Labiche had made his name. But with the advent of Alexandre Dumas *fils* comedy of the simple kind inaugurated by Picard, with its tendency to melodrama and to vaudeville, gave way to the modern serious comedy of the Romantic school, realistically staged, which counted Augier and Sardou among its supporters.

The Romantic spirit, made national in France by Chateaubriand, affected the drama of the period in two definite directions. First it encouraged the presentation on the stage of historical drama, the setting of the Middle Ages being especially popular : and this brought about a revolution in dress, accessories, and scenery, which were elaborated with all the archæological knowledge that was then available. An example of such a play was Delavigne's *Charles VII* : which was mainly a spectacle, reproducing scenes from mediæ-

---

[1] A similar change was made by Kotzebue in Germany, whose plays, though not literary, were popular all over Europe.

[2] Perhaps the most important serious plays of this period were an *Attila* which in 1824 reflected the patriotic sense of France in finding herself delivered for the time from the German soldiery ; the early historical plays of Casimir Delavigne ; *Sylla* by Jouy in 1821, aimed at Napoleon I, and *Regulus* by Arnault, an attack on England.

val life, war, the sport of falconry, single combats,
and so on. Secondly, there was a desire among the
Romantic dramatists, including such different temperaments as De Musset, Victor Hugo, and De Vigny,
to strike out for freedom of method. In Victor
Hugo's case this meant an attack upon, and a destruction of, classic form as then understood, and in every
case it meant that a background, foreign or exotic,
remote in time or experience, was used, upon which
the action of the play developed. The famous " bataille " for the recognition of Hugo's methods in *Hernani*
marked the turning-point, after which freedom was
assured to the dramatist. But the author's liberty
of action does not always imply that the general
public will accept all his ideas. De Musset's first
plays failed to please, original and delicate in treatment as they were, and their success was delayed
till a later date. Hugo, too, failed to command the
attention of his audience in his later plays, though
they were staged with emphasis on spectacular effect
and on rapid and surprising developments in the
action.

As distinct from the great dramatists of the seventeenth century, the Romantic playwrights in France
tended to make theories of dramatic construction,
instead of allowing theories to be elicited from the
" chef-d'œuvres " of the period. Theory too frequently was unsupported by successful practice.
Victor Hugo's *Préface de Cromwell*, with its bold
argument for the use of the grotesque element in drama,
and in fact for the use of every element either used by
Shakespeare (to whom all the Romantics professed
allegiance) or found in ordinary life, was an appeal
against the formal machinery of play-writing, and an
incentive to the creation of new forms, which was,
however, hardly supported by the play to which it

was attached.   It was the battle-cry of one generation only.

A more telling exposition of dramatic theory is, however, found in the work of a critic of the early Romantic period, G. Desjardins,[1] who was not himself a playwright.   His argument is interesting because of his understanding of and sympathy with the form of the Greek and of the French classic drama : while he suggests a new formula for construction that would include a variety of new " genres."   He begins by stating that in all drama there is an undercurrent of feeling which is in opposition to some of the acts of man and supports others.   It gives the promise of conflict, of resistance before this appears in action.

" Les trois premiers actes, en préparant l'agression, ne feraient donc, tout au plus, que nous promettre un drame sans nous le donner . . . si à travers le développement de la crainte et des terreurs, presque toutes *speculatives*, des premiers actes, ne se glissait, comme inaperçue, une puissance d'opposition et de défense, puissance sourde, occulte, d'autant plus grande et plus terrible, qu'on en apprécie moins d'abord les proportions ;   puissance d'opposition (ainsi que dans Saül) quelquefois incommensurable comme la Divinité, sur laquelle elle s'appuie, opposition qui, née de l'espérance, a besoin, pour nous plaire, d'apparaître dans les premiers actes vague et indéfinie comme elle."

The action of the play, the sense of unseen forces and the background of opposition are brought into connexion by some external shock which puts facts into focus and produces the dramatic crisis.   This gives the play its " social significance," and sets the characters in a new relation to one another ; a relation which is controlled by one main idea.   Thus the play is " social " in the sense that the shock affects all the characters nearly concerned in the plot.

[1] Review of Soumet's *Saul*.   *Muse Française*, 1824, ed. Marsan, t. 1, p. 129.

" Oui, le drame vient de recevoir la vie, car une suite de faits qui s'enchaînent, l'eût-on étendue aux cinq actes, n'eût pas plus constitué un *drame* et donné à des êvènemens un mode particulier d'existence, que, si j'ose m'exprimer ainsi, la plupart de nos modernes agglomérations d'hommes ne constituent une patrie, ne réalisent cet être moral et collectif qui domine et plane sur toutes les individualités, et fait que tous, avec des interêts distincts, respirent en commun, se lèvent, agissent *comme un seul homme* et par une même pensée."

This criticism is significant not only in what is said, but in what is left out. It is assumed throughout that the subconscious influences are external to the drama of human life, but wake echoes in it. They are conceived of as belonging to a larger world, definitely controlled by a Power, and on the whole the subconscious influences of which Desjardins thinks are really the indication of man's higher, not his lower nature. This was in accordance with the general tone of thought at the time he wrote. The arena has been considerably enlarged since 1823. Plays are now written in which man is seen to struggle with a better subconscious nature, or sometimes with a worse. The central fact which gives these plays a unity of conception is that of conflict.

Desjardins then appears to stand between the theorists of the seventeenth century and the individualists of the nineteenth. His theory combines the social element in Corneille with the mysterious element in Racine,[1] and thus prepares the way for a new development. We must also add that theorizing on the past practice of the stage, he described the type of French classical tragedy which, under the influence of Shake-

[1] The social element was, however, not wanting to Racine : his dislike of the usually received Greek plot of the *Iphigenia* was due to his sense of the impossibility of presenting to a French audience a play in which the daughter is sacrificed by her father.

speare, was worked out at the end of the eighteenth
century in the plays of Marie-Joseph Chénier and
Nepomucène Lemercier. We should expect the formula he discovered to be derived from a study of
Shakespeare's *Hamlet*, which play greatly affected both
these authors [1] and an examination of which is important to the argument. Hamlet's conflict is one between
his instinctive knowledge of facts, which brings with
it a necessity for action, and the absence of rational
proof of his mother's and uncle's actual guilt. When
the proof is discovered (though neither in *Hamlet*
nor in *Lear* can we say that the truth emerges through
a fact external to the hero, rather in each case the
test is engineered by the central character) the crisis
occurs. This is in the play scene (one left out by Ducis
in his adaptation) ; and all the characters as a consequence fall into dramatic relation with Hamlet. In
the light of his painful certainty his relation is altered
to Ophelia—he slays Polonius, dismisses his friends,
and only keeps a very modified connexion with Hor-
atio. Here we find in all probability the germ of
Desjardins' formula, which can be applied with equal
success to Shakespeare's other tragedies, to Greek
drama, and to the French tragic drama of the seventeenth century.

In one point Desjardins agreed with all French critics
of tragedy. The eighteenth-century writers observed
that the effect of a tragedy is moral, and though they
did not see altogether clearly how that came about,
it is evident to a later generation that the high tone
of all seventeenth-century tragedy came from the strong
conviction held by French tragic writers of that date
that the good in the world must ultimately prevail.
They cared intensely, too, that the good should pre-

[1] Le Tourneur's translation of Shakespeare began to appear
in 1776.

vail. Thus there emerged moral as well as artistic values in drama. A nation that has convictions and beliefs has the material for tragedy. The play that is the expression of despair or carelessness can only succeed if it is a criticism of life, and if the contrast is made between real life and the elements chosen out for portrayal on the stage. This kind of play leans to melodrama or to farce and has not the force of genuine tragedy. Possibly for these reasons Romantic drama has not given us great tragedy. There was uncertainty of aim in both political and individual life, and this uncertainty caused Romantic drama to be a series of experiments in which the tendency was to melodrama. Examples of incomplete form due to the uncertainty of aim of the author can be freely found in the nineteenth century in France. Victor Hugo made the weakness of his heroes actually weaken the meshes of the plot. Alfred de Vigny in the preface to *Chatterton* explained that he left out everything in the life of his hero which was inconsistent with the main idea of the author.[1] But in some modern plays there is a combination of realistic treatment in detail with true dramatic significance and unity : and where this occurs[2] the author has tried the experiment foreshadowed by Racine and Maeterlinck, and admitted by Desjardins as a possible type of drama : he has given to the conscious acts of his characters a setting of unconscious impulses, of feelings which never rise into action, of waves which disturb but never break, and the remarkable intensity of repressed feelings forms a background upon which the most ordinary words can acquire dramatic value.

[1] *Dernière nuit de travail.* " Je viens d'écarter à dessein des faits exacts de sa vie pour ne prendre de sa destinée que ce qui la rend un exemple à jamais déplorable d'une noble misère."
[2] As for example in Miss Sowerby's *Rutherford and Son.*

From the new standpoint reached in the early years of the nineteenth century it became possible to classify the dramatic types which appeared before that time with some relation to the new order of ideas. Ferdinand Brunetière produced what is perhaps the simplest and most comprehensive definition of drama. He described all drama as concerned with the conflict of the will, and he made the force and sincerity of that conflict account for every type of drama from tragedy to farce. But the view of the critic of 1823-4 was even larger in that he saw the possibility of dramatic unity in plays in which the consciousness of the conflict is shared or for the time obscured. If we apply this theory it will be found to include plays outside the regular classical form of the seventeenth century, together with the mixed "genres" and attempts at novel forms which were characteristic of the eighteenth. The two theories do not contradict one another, but Desjardins admits a further problem, that of the psychology of consciousness, into the drama.[1]

The new spirit on the stage found its greatest exponents in two men of very different calibre—Alfred de Musset and Victor Hugo.

Alfred de Musset's plays are examples of a new spirit in French literature—but as the first were not successful on the stage, and the later ones were written

[1] It is possible that the social idea in the drama is directly responsible for this. For if tragedy is conceived of as illustrating the attack upon personality leading to its loss or destruction, comedy may be thought of as showing the justifiable moulding of character and habits to fit a person to take his place in society. In the first case cruel suffering is the part of a person whose ideal is above that of the society round him, or differs from it ; in the second case a person is forced for his own advantage into a social groove in matters relatively unessential.

without a view to immediate production, they did
not influence the practice of the stage till the period
1860–70. In these plays a background of stage
scenery is as unnecessary as it was to the seventeenth-
century classical drama. And this was because the
central interest was sufficiently strong to need no
external support. On the other hand, De Musset's
drama both demanded and produced atmosphere,
through a series of characters introduced for that
purpose. Thus a dramatic perspective takes the place
of an elaborate setting.[1] In manipulating the technique of his plays, De Musset obtained considerable
variety of effect by contrast of character and situation. The grotesque element appears, for example
in the chorus of *On ne badine pas avec l'amour*,
while the figures in the chorus are yet less psychologically real than the central characters to which they
form a background. The element of surprise is one
which De Musset knew how to handle, and whether
this is tragic, as in *On ne badine pas avec l'amour*, or
comic, as in *On ne saurait penser à tout*, it produces the
effect of reality in a play in which anything may
happen, and where the events are not staged according to the conventions of the theatre.

The truth of De Musset's art is shown in the experience of presenting the plays, for they have not always
been staged with the costumes and scenery appropriate
to their actual date, and yet, when these have been
consistent with themselves, the effect has been pleasing.
The fact of the uncertain direction of emotional impulse,·
one used by Racine, is familiar to De Musset, whose
work exhibits both the social play of characters in
relation to one another, and the growing tendencies
of human beings to come together or to fall apart,

---

[1] Songs and music contribute to the atmosphere in many
of the plays.

which are made visible to the audience even where
the impulse is scarcely strong enough to change the
plot and general disposition of the play. The complexity of the main characters, who show this
inner and outer movement of their feeling, is balanced by the simplicity of the minor characters, a
simplicity which has the elements of caricature, or at
times of the art of the poster, where the artistic effect
is produced by few lines and a narrow scale of tones.

The other great Romantic experiment, that of
Victor Hugo, has little in common with De Musset's
except the deliberate inclusion of grotesque types.
Where De Musset liberates the imagination by increasing the varieties of psychological experience which he
stages, Hugo does so by including a large number of
unusual events, generally with little coherence and
connexion.

The difference in mind and character between the
two men largely accounts for this contrast in their
art. De Musset's development made him acquainted
with every variety of emotional pain and pleasure ;
and this experience is placed as a whole on the stage.
Hugo with all his brilliance and force could not give
a definite direction to his art nor give to his plays the
whole value of his own development. " Je suis une
force qui va," is his own definition of his quality. To
the French mind, which, with all its richness and versa-
tility, desires and obtains an even development and
a sense of purpose in life, the dramas of Victor Hugo
are a confession of failure. Thus every device of
dramatic contrast and of picturesque scenery is used
by Victor Hugo in order to make his play stand firmly,
for the characters repeat his own uncertainty of aim,
and the plot is in consequence loosely woven and not
shaped to any decided end. And yet the work of
Hugo was extremely important in the development

of stage conditions, for it marked the entrance of melodrama into serious work in obedience to the desire for excitement which is noticeable in any country after a period of revolution or of war. It also marks a desire to make language telling and topical instead of stilted or conventional, and thus nearer to modern ways. As far as possible, Hugo produced this change within the limits of the poetical drama. But a new and slightly bizarre effect is produced on a stage where the art of speech is rendered as naturally as possible, while scenery and costume are of the imagined date of the play. The symbolism of verse had broken down, but not the symbolism of setting. In this way Hugo initiated a dramatic method which dominated the nineteenth century and has only been replaced as lately as the present century by different theories both in regard to setting and language. The background of Hugo's plays is always romantic, that is a different " milieu," or a different period from the present, furnishes his inspiration. Sometimes, as in *Ruy Blas*, he succeeds in painting an historical picture, but he succeeds at the expense of form and construction in the play. The audience can find much to enjoy in the poetry, and in the vigour of the adventures described, so long as the dramatic sense is not critical.

The greatest criticism of the Romantic stage is its history. It has had in France no real succession : it has formed no school. It carried on, it is true, a tradition that plays could be founded on national events : that tradition had been formed by Chénier and Lemercier : it competed with the Opera in the variety of its scenic changes and the restlessness of its course : it stood for freedom of expression. But not one of these points belongs to the essentials of dramatic art. Great actors and actresses demanded classical tragedy for the development of their powers, and in fact there was a revival of classical tragedy in France after the excitement caused by the performance of *Hernani* had subsided. The plays have become a part of the literature of the past instead of a present experience, they have been reproduced and well staged, and in this way have been an excellent lesson to the present generation on the subject of the Romantic drama. But they survive rather as a part of the history of literature than as living drama.

While the plays of Goethe and Schiller in Germany had a certain epic quality and were remarkable also for lyric force, the plays of the French Romantics suggest the structure of the historical novel rather than that of compact drama : they thus derive their structure as well as their inspiration to a large extent from Scott.

It is generally understood that the Napoleonic domination of Europe helped to turn the direction of German dramatic work after Schiller towards the "Schicksal's tragödie" or fate-drama. Schiller's *Die Braut von Messina* was the archetype of many other plays, with this difference, that Schiller had attempted to recover with doubtful success the Greek notion of destiny, but his followers in the "genre" substituted a mediæval form of superstition for the Greek. The continuous influence of Shakespeare on the German stage is thus explained : Shakespeare is perpetually conscious of the belief of the crowd in fate—as instanced by the stars "that govern our conditions"—

"When these prodigies,
Do so conjointly meet, let not men say
'These are their reasons, they are natural'" [1]

and the plays of Shakespeare in which Fate openly

[1] *Julius Cæsar*, Act I, sc. 3.

plays a part, *Macbeth* and *Hamlet*, were especially
influential at this period.[1]

The fate-motive in the newer form was developed
by Werner, Tieck, and others, and appears again in
Grillparzer, whose work needs special notice.

The tendency of the fate-drama had been to insti-
tute a new division of the play into acts or scenes
which were rigidly marked out by certain fateful
anniversaries.[2] The construction of the German play
was improved by this fact ; and by the relation of
the whole play to the crisis.

Grillparzer (1791–1872) wrote the last important
fate-tragedy, *Die Ahnfrau*, in 1817, and his work shows
superior constructional force. He used a trochaic

[1] Schiller had just translated *Macbeth* before writing *Die
Braut von Messina*.

The influence of *Macbeth* on the German stage is well
known. The device of a sleep-walking scene was used by
Kleist, in *Der Prinz von Homburg*. Here the author uses
the incident to show that the hero of the play has a weak
side to his nature ; and the course of the play demonstrates
the result.

Kleist's version of the story of *Amphitryon* stresses this
peculiarity of a second self, in contrast to the more traditional
version in which Molière adapted the story to the court life
of Louis XIV.

Another effect which was imitated from Shakespeare was
the device of the play within the play. The play scene in
Hamlet has a significance in the plot, but it also aids the stage
illusion. Tieck makes the fullest use of the device, by providing an audience on the stage and making their comments
a part of the play. In *Die Verkehrte Welt* he makes some
of the characters consider themselves an audience and refer
to the actual audience in the theatre. The questionings of
Hamlet, his indecision, and the doubt about his sanity and
purpose, reappear on the stage in Germany, where the " Dop-
pelgänger," or vision of the self, appears to complete the
character as it does in French Romantic verse (see De Musset,
Nuit de Décembre) and in the *Tales of Hoffman*.

[2] As in Werner's *Der Vierundzwanzigste Februar*.

metre, which produced the effect of an incantation.
The metre is varied by a song and choric interludes.
The scenery is described with care and definiteness,
showing that a story of superstition had to have a
convincing background (including effects of stage
lightning) to seem in the least probable.   The scenery
remains the same for four acts and is only changed
for the crisis.

This play was succeeded by a number of others of
different types.   These were affected as much by
contemporary political movements as were M. J.
Chénier's in France, and thus are to a large extent
political and historical documents.   But a remarkable
trilogy, based upon the story of the Golden Fleece
(*Das Goldene Vliess*) is one of the best attempts in
the modern period to recapture the largeness of the
Greek spirit.

Both the plays of Grillparzer and Hebbel (1813–
63) (who worked out the idea of tragedy on simple
lines, and thus instituted the modern social drama),
were performed in Vienna, where the life of the drama
and the allied arts survived more completely than
in other German-speaking countries, though with even
less encouragement from the Government.

After the Franco-German War of 1870 the centre
of German dramatic art was Berlin, now the capital
of the Empire.   Here were produced the " bourgeois "
tragedies of Sudermann and the imaginative work of
Hauptmann, whose love of realistic detail allied to
a symbolic treatment of the story (as in *Die Versunkene
Glocke*, 1897) called upon all the resources of the
modern stage for its adequate representation.

CHAPTER VIII

THE MODERN PERIOD

(d) THE PRESENT DAY

THE first half of the nineteenth century, though including in France the work of the Romantic dramatists, and the development of Opera in Italy, France, Germany, and England (in England light Opera was more congenial than grand Opera),[1] produced no fresh examination of the relation between a play and its setting on the stage. But in the latter part of the century two new and important experiments in drama were made : one had a Scandinavian source, in Ibsen, and another, in Maeterlinck, drew inspiration from French art. Working with opposed tendencies, both writers obtained original and effective results. Both had the setting of a play in mind as part of the total expressiveness of their art.

Ibsen deliberately cuts out all romantic interest from his drama. This leads him to set his stage with a realism that is a development from the French stage of the eighteenth century. He concentrates his attention very largely on a scene in a house which

---

[1] See the Introduction to Gay's *Beggar's Opera* a hundred years earlier where the same note was struck. " I hope I may be forgiven that I have not made my Opera throughout unnatural, like those in vogue: for I have no Recitative; excepting this, as I have consented to have neither prologue nor epilogue, it must be allowed an opera in all its forms."

has an outlet on to a garden, and another exit to an inner living-room. All his characters live, as it were, on the brink of some new development, and this is symbolized when they go out by the garden door, either into the world or into a despairing solitude.

The setting of the stage is uncompromisingly realistic. The object of his drama is to show in the narrowest and most familiar surroundings the working out of a problem which is world-wide in its application. It is not surprising that the machinery creaks and the frame bends in the process. The intensity of the drama is at times difficult to bear without the necessary artistic relief. The setting is so inadequate to the strength of the emotions in the characters that it would only be tolerable if the scenery were plain and symbolic, and not realistic. The meaning outweighs the setting. But Ibsen is not satisfied without dictating the pattern of the carpet and the position of every chair.

Maeterlinck desired, too, to show the unseen reality which exists all about us and is hidden by material facts. In order to make his presentation convincing, he robs the daylight-existence of all life and character and individuality. People become instruments of a hidden life and hidden forces. They are veiled and shrouded, and so is their speech. The effect is what he desired, but it is so remote from ordinary life that the problem fails to grip us. The setting outweighs the meaning, through its strange difference from the world we know.

When these groups of plays found producers who looked at drama from the point of view of stage craft, new possibilities, however, presented themselves. The Moscow Art theatre, one of the most interesting theatrical experiments before the war, dealt with any play in which unseen forces dominated humanity, by raising the height of the stage opening. Men were then dwarfed by the picture, though not rendered vague.

Maeterlinck's *Blue Bird* has been staged in London
in this way. When, however, as in Ibsen's plays
and some of Tchekoff's, it is intended that human
life shall be the dominating interest, then the stage
opening is widened and lowered. The characters
stand out in contrast to their background and control
the play. On the other hand, the depth of the stage
from front to back is lessened in Maeterlinck's drama,
and increased for Ibsen's and Tchekoff's. The reason
for this is to be found in the spirit of the plays. With
Maeterlinck the symbolic presentation becomes at
times like pageantry, where the eye is occupied only
with one stream or moving group. Characters follow
one another on to the stage, producing indeed variety
in a certain order, but not perspective in action. In
Ibsen's plays the complexity of life as he imagines it
is illustrated by the opportunity for by-play and side
actions which do not necessarily illustrate the main
action, but serve to point out the many conflicting
issues of the play, any one of which may at any time
become prominent. There is, however, reason for
narrowing the stage in Maeterlinck's drama,[1] for by

[1] See Bakshy, *The Path of the Modern Russian Stage* (p.
61) : "The object of Maeterlinck in his plays is to reveal
the inner mysteries of life by making the audience experience
them as actual facts. His ambition is to break down the
barrier between the stage and the audience and cause the
performance to become a kind of religious service in which
the individuality of the spectator merges into some sublime
vision of the inner world. The solution of this problem
offered by Meyerhold does great credit to his sense of the
theatrical form. He staged Maeterlinck's dramas on one
plane, i.e. he reduced the depth of the stage to a narrow
band close to the footlights and placed the actors against
flat decorative scenery, aiming thereby to dematerialize the
stage and to merge the action of the play in the sway of
emotions felt by the audience. . . . Nothing is so capable
of destroying the opposition between the spectator and the
object observed as the perception of a flat surface."

bringing the actors closer to the audience and eliminating a background, the audience are able to share more closely in the emotional situation of the characters on the stage. Maeterlinck wishes the audience to identify itself with the situation.[1] Ibsen, on the other hand, considers that the audience should play the part of spectator and judge. For his plays have a distinct moral purpose which goes home with greater effect where the identification between actors and audience is not complete.

It will be observed that when Granville Barker, under the influence of the Moscow Art theatre, gave his mind to the modern staging of Shakespeare's plays, he obtained his effect by using flat scenery, against which the living actors gained in vividness and force. This can be illustrated by his production of *Twelfth Night*.

Other experiments recently made have been planned on similar lines. In the Oxford representation of Hardy's *The Dynasts* (1920) [2] the flat curtain of linen, painted in a childishly symbolic way, served the purpose of throwing the interest on the actors. Where the human interest of the play overwhelmed the fate-motive, as in the scene at Salamanca and the scene in the cock-pit of the *Victory*, and that in which Napoleon appeared at Fontainebleau, the height-measurement of the stage opening was lessened. To a lesser degree the simplicity of the one adapted room

[1] It is worth while to notice here that Reinhardt's great production of *Œdipus Rex* at Covent Garden failed in one particular. Following the German version of an Elizabethan tradition, the blinded king was made to stagger out to exile through the audience—as Richard II had done. But here Greek feeling was lost ; for Œdipus on the Greek stage fell back in his misery into the shadow of the house. It was his loss of contact with the audience, not the increased contact, that fitted the emotional need of that last scene.

[2] Produced by Mr. Granville Barker.

in Drinkwater's *Abraham Lincoln* also contributed to the same effect, though the simplicity was at times marred by stage furniture.

There have been two other interesting experiments of late years in which at certain points the two worlds —real and symbolic—are effectively combined on the stage. In Rostand's *Chantecler* the birds occupy a wide stage, not too high, and they are of gigantic size. In the last act the legs of the gamekeeper are seen, immediately reducing the world of the birds to a relation with the human world we know.

In the Bath Passion Play in 1920, in order to avoid the representation of Christ on the stage, which in this country is against the law, the final scene shows the feet of the crucified Christ just visible at the top of the stage opening, and the episodes at the foot of the Cross are thus put into relation with the Divine story and with another world beyond the stage-world.[1]

So short a time has elapsed since the Great War of 1914–18 that the relation between the stage and life has not yet had a full opportunity of adjusting itself. The war was followed in all European countries, and particularly in France, with her strong dramatic consciousness, by a reaction on the one hand to melodrama, and on the other to symbolic plays.[2] Musical comedy and spy-stories were popular in England, but France, except in the most critical period of the war, also admitted classical plays and serious comedy. The tendency was to produce short plays (such, for instance, as those used in the " Théâtre des Armées ").

There are two directions in which dramatic art

[1] The law on this subject in England has codified a mediæval custom, in which, for the sake of reverence, the whole figure of the crucified Christ was not exhibited on the mystery stage.

[2] Such as *Les Cathédrales*.

may possibly move. Representations may become more definitely romantic in character, with the intention of amusing or pleasing an audience already used to the cinema. This would make for rapid changes of scenery, variety in the plot, and little character-drawing. On the other hand, plays may be written to appeal to a literary and cultivated audience, such as that which attends a repertory theatre. In such cases the difficulties of financing the plays will lead to economy in the presentation and simplification of scenery : the interest being focused by good actors on plot and character development. Should such a national drama follow the lead of Ibsen, the interest will be restricted to certain problems of a certain period : because only a problem which is both temporary and acute in its character, a social problem, that is, which is on the way to being solved, will retain the interest of a large audience. Such plays will have the character of realism, but in a very few years their performance will demand from the audience the same qualities of imagination that lead us to look on at a play by Ibsen and attempt to take the interest in it that was taken at the time of its first representation.[1]

It is given to few modern dramatists to transcend this method, but certain studies of social life such as *Le Maître des Forges* (represented in England as *The Iron Master*), Henri Bataille's studies of the demi-monde, such as *La Possession*, awake an intensity of feeling which lifts the play on to the level of great drama. The plays of Bernard Shaw have no such quality : the romantic and the critical elements live the life of an ill-assorted couple in his drama, and his work will live mainly as a clever picture of a passing phase of society. Galsworthy's plays—

[1] For an illustration of this point note the partial success of the revival of *The Second Mrs. Tanqueray*.

especially *Strife*, *The Silver Box*, and, recently, *Loyalties*—do, however, belong to the finer category. So too do the plays of Drinkwater, for dealing for the most part with historical characters, as for example *Abraham Lincoln*, these plays succeed in convincing a modern audience that the ideal moves about in human life in the garb of the real. In the setting of such plays emphasis is rightly laid by the producer on the life-like but worn elements in appearance and scenery, for thus an effect of greater contrast is produced between the shining human spirit and the fatigued body and the cumbering material world in which it moves.

There is now no art of the stage which can be said to be generally applicable. The production of a play is a fact in which author, actors, and the makers of setting and scenery must collaborate, or else failure in art will be the result. But given these conditions, the playwright is neither hampered by the stage nor inspired by his opportunities—he makes his setting in imagination and forms his actors as he writes the play, and so far as he can combine the effects he desires, his drama has an individual existence as a work of art.

The combination presents great difficulties, as however original the quality of the playwright's art, he has to face traditions of production and scenery, which are only just yielding to a desire for greater simplification of background, and traditions of the actor's art that fetter the imagination and reduce expression to a formula. Let us suppose that a playwright has in his mind a comedy of social life. If it is intended to show various facets of a social problem, not only the principal characters but the subsidiary ones must be alive, and must gain the attention of the onlookers by an appeal from them to a problem on the stage which is of significance to all, as in Galsworthy's *Loyalties*. The actors must be able to convince every one of the reality of that appeal. They must live, and forget everything but the life of the characters they represent and the audience which is being addressed.

If the play is intended to present a purely individual experience, something of a different type is possible. The secondary characters need only contribute to our knowledge of the central character. Their gestures and words may be selected for that purpose, and should be arresting, but not necessarily expressive of the personality of the speakers. A play of this type by George Kaiser was produced in 1920 by the Stage Society under the name of *From Morn till Midnight*. In both types of play simplicity of setting is a necessity.

It should be noticed in considering the setting of a modern play, that the position of the scenery and background on the stage frequently suggest that the stage-world is set at an angle in relation to the auditorium. This produces variety and depth in the setting, and exits and entrances can be arranged to appear more natural. The audience, mainly facing the stage, therefore sees it as a person seated in the side gallery of an Elizabethan theatre would have seen it, thus apparently gaining a view of the depth of the stage from back to front.

In the matter of changes of scene, recent experiments with a revolving stage in which three or possibly more scenes can be substituted one for another, have proved very suitable to the staging of plays in which long waits between the scenes tend to break the thread of the illusion. They are for the same reason suitable to plays in which the stage events happen within a very limited time. This is a large and intricate modern development of a method of which the Greek "periaktoi" or revolving screens gave the first early indication.

APPENDIX I

VERSIONS OF GREEK STORIES

AN examination of the genealogy of the persons, real and legendary, who are characters in the ancient Greek drama brings out the fact that stories of unwilling or " sinless " crime are connected with one group of persons, derived from the family of the Theban kings. Stories of wilful or unprovoked crime, leading to the tragedy of a whole family and to a curse which has to be expiated, are connected with the offspring of Poseidon, standing for the " dark waters " of legend and for the restless and unmastered sea. Persons half human, half divine, such as Herakles, with characteristics of the " sons of God," belong through Zeus to the family of Kronos and of Rhea. Characters degraded by association with animals, such as Phædra (offspring of the union of Minos and Pasiphæ), come into the genealogy through some unknown and barbarian source, therefore subject to suspicion. Characters such as Medea possessing the witches' power and more than a suspicion of madness, also come from the barbarian lands from which the Hellenes had withdrawn themselves.

We have to look, then, beyond history and known legend for some explanation of this very complete organization of the characters in Greek drama.

The fear of the " dark waters," which appears in all folk-myth, goes back farther than the very limited floods recorded in Babylonian and Hebraic legend. In fact some elements in the description of a local waste of waters clearly refer to an older and more complete change of conditions either climatic, when the sun was shrouded and ice fastened up the " fresh waters," and deprived the earth of the power of fertilization, or the result of migration of a land people to an island civilization. In the Babylonian lament for Tammuz this is described as the absence of the Sun-god. In the Indian Rig-Veda the thanksgiving hymns for the reappearance of the sun and the freeing of the rivers from the " darkness on the face of the deep " were acted as well as sung, and were the foundations for Indian drama. The same mythological events are repeated in the Hittite and Egyptian records.

Greek mythology takes up the same story and shows the ensuing conflict between Zeus, lord of the sky and of life, and of the opposing forces :—the Titans, who attacked high Heaven, and the progeny of Poseidon, including also the serpents and other creatures located in " dark waters." This accounts for a large number of Greek dramatic plots. Some other origins must be sought for in a different direction.

In the history of the hero, half human and half divine, in the Greek mythology (represented by Herakles and by the legend of Demeter and Persephone) we have a drama not only of death but of resurrection. The myths of sunrise and sunset, of spring and autumn, foreshadow a deep belief in the immortality of the human spirit. In the Greek drama the story of Alkestis, into which Herakles enters as an actor, has the clearest reference to this ancient belief. Alkestis is herself descended from Deucalion, who is connected with the Greek story of a local flood.

The root origins of the art of the Greek drama were perhaps clearer in ancient Greece than they are to a modern over-sophisticated world. Yet in re-telling and re-dramatizing these old stories it is interesting to see how each generation has seized on those elements in the stories

that were needed for the spiritual help of the generation
to which the authors belonged.[1]

The relation of a plot to its staging, to the supernatural
characters, and to the use of the chorus can be perhaps
best studied in the historical development of a play or
group of plays, from ancient to modern times.[2]

(1) THE EUMENIDES

In the trilogy of Æschylus, consisting of the *Agamemnon*,
the *Chœphori*, and the *Eumenides*, the last play has survived in the most clear and consistent form. We can
gather from the text the following facts about the staging
of the play.

It moves with very little interruption from the beginning
to the end. But there are two breaks, by means of which
the play is divided into three acts. Of these breaks, which
mark a change of scene in the play, one at least is shown
to coincide with the clearing of the characters off the stage.
Probably therefore there was a convention by which the
characters were removed before a change of scene. Choric
odes fill the interval. No local allusions are found in this
play, thus anything attempted in the way of scenery would
have been of the simplest nature. Though at this date
the action probably took place in the orchestra, there
may have been a temple frontage on the *scena* in Act I,
and in Act II an altar, a house, and an image of Athena.
Apollo, as a local deity, appeared above the Temple.
Orestes surrounded by the Erinyes may have been brought
forward to form a tableau on a movable platform.

Æschylus seems to have used the very moderate possi-

[1] The later legends of the fall of man and the story of Cain,
as affecting the tragic drama, are referred to in Appendix II.
For the references in both appendixes I am indebted to some
unpublished notes on the Book of Genesis by Miss C. A. E.
Moberly, and to Miss Weston, *From Ritual to Romance*.

[2] The method of this study was suggested by notes in
Jebb's edition of Sophocles, and I acknowledge a debt to
that author for many suggestions in regard to the Greek
plays mentioned. Further material has been added to complete the argument.

bilities of the stage of his day in a remarkable way. He introduced new elements into the drama. Such were the Furies, with their realistic presentation of the perversion of the winged creature, and their emphasis on its destructive character. Such again was the ghost. The life after death, though conceived of as a shrunken life, and the presence of the Divine forces, both local and general, are thus shown by Æschylus in symbolic form.

Sophocles, in treating the same subject, gives the supernatural a place in the design of the play, but concentrates interest on the human aspect of his drama. His gods and goddesses become necessarily more decorative and less influential. He does not use the Erinyes as an influence in the plot, but gives the part to Apollo, and though he brings the gods less on the stage, Sophocles refers to them more often than do Æschylus or Euripides. Euripides further reduces the element of Divine action, and causes his gods to utter narrative speeches as prologue and epilogue.

The use of the chorus is another characteristic by which we can distinguish the work of the Greek tragedian. Æschylus not only creates the Furies but identifies them with the chorus. Sophocles makes no such great change, but he introduces a perpetual interaction between the actors and chorus, and between the chorus and the audience. Without manipulating the stage or altering its character, he connects the audience with a complicated action in the play. In Euripides the chorus is a lyrical addition to the play, but not a part of the action.

When we study the Roman play we find that in Seneca's use of the same topics for drama the parts of the supernatural are further restricted. Unquestionably the Roman attitude was more sceptical than the Greek. Gods and goddesses were purely decorative and there were a large number of mute characters, whose rôle was also merely decorative. Where a ghost was introduced, it was often referred to in narrative and there was not a direct introduction of the character. The ghost body reproduces the wounds or other characters of the living body.

Seneca used gods and spirits to speak his prologues. This removed any necessity for tiers of staging in the Roman theatre, where one high platform only was provided.

When Racine dealt with Greek plots, he identified the god of Greek tragedy with some force of nature, suitable to his conception, and thus he obtained a unity of effect. For example in *Phèdre*, the means of destruction wrought by Neptune are the waves of the sea and the sea monster. In *Iphigénie*, when the curse is removed, the gods accept the sacrifice with fire from heaven and Diana ascends in a cloud. In order to fit in with the exigencies of the French stage, the events are merely reported and not presented.

(2) ŒDIPUS TYRANNUS

As an example of the effect of plot and character-drawing on the use made of the stage, the drama of Œdipus will be a convenient one to examine.

This subject was treated by Æschylus, and his scheme is known to us, by Sophocles, and by Euripides, but only fragments survive of the last play. All agree in their account of the relationship of Œdipus and Jocasta, and of the curse of Œdipus on the two sons.

Æschylus had written a trilogy in which the *Œdipus* was the central part. Some words only survive of the *Laius*, the earlier play, and some verses of the *Œdipus*. In these, however, we have an account of Œdipus blinding himself and calling down the curse on his sons. The last part of the trilogy, the *Seven Against Thebes*, is extant.

All we can gather from the remains of Æschylus' play is that the discovery of Œdipus' crime is brought about by mechanical devices and recognitions. It is the fate-*motif* struggling for expression in conventional ways; and it needs no special stage-setting.

Sophocles, however, gives us a complete play : and the climax here is not the curse, with the premonition of after consequences, but the discovery of the crime. This is brought about in two ways, ingeniously combined. Œdipus is said to have been given to the herdman of

Polybus, King of Corinth, by the Theban herd of Laius. He gets to know of his own parentage, but the terrible significance of it is hidden from him, though apparent to the audience. We have thus a larger play with a delayed crisis. The action is in a world unknown to the audience. Sophocles takes out the Furies, the dominant influence in the early play, and transfers this influence to Apollo, the punisher of impurity, thus giving the play a moral meaning. He chooses for the scene of Œdipus' encounter with his father the three roads near Daulis which were within the range of Apollo's influence at Delphi.

The attitude of the chorus—not now the Furies, but the citizens of Thebes—is changed. These citizens are human, and express the natural feeling of a crowd. They resent the evil fate falling on an unconscious sinner : but they blame Œdipus for being arrogant to Creon, and Jocasta for disbelieving the oracle. They look forward with joy to the proof of Œdipus' royal birth. The chorus in this play exhibits many elements of the subconscious crowd-mind. It foretells the probable impression on the people of each successive event, and makes the stage action seem less unlikely and mechanical.

There were, of course, in Sophocles' play as in Æschylus' some very improbable elements in the plot. These are, however, all in the antecedents, and Aristotle notices that in this way the best dramatic practice is followed. Here Aristotle touches on a real fact in the human nature of the theatre-goer, the onlooker accepts quite easily any improbable supposition provided that this particular part of the story is not acted in his presence.[1]

Sophocles, in the play before us, shows a fear of moral anarchy, and also expresses his own lack of faith in earlier stories of the action of the gods. It is the exercise of a

---

[1] An illustration of this fact can be found in Shakespeare. It is not likely, though possible, that in a shipwreck a ship would divide exactly in two, leaving one of two pairs of twins in each half. Such an event could not be acted in the *Comedy of Errors*, but was assumed as an antecedent to the play, and caused no difficulty in a lively and otherwise realistic comedy.

relentless logic that brings Œdipus to abase himself before the gods ; he does not accept the view of prophet or interpreter. Hence his sceptical attitude to Teiresias.

In Seneca's treatment of the same play we find rather a compressed and much more rationalist and realistic version of the Greek drama.

(a) Teiresias practises incantations, like the Roman priest, to discover the murderer, and calls up Laius from the shades. This, however, is a scene related to the main plot. It is a scene that on the Greek stage would have been a part of the action.

(b) After the discovery of Œdipus' crime, Jocasta, rigid with horror, kills herself on the stage. In Sophocles' version she is unable to bear the terrible truth and rushes away in a frenzy of despair.

(c) Œdipus goes into voluntary exile. He and Jocasta have dealt separately and independently with their lives. There is no softening touch such as the recognition of the children in the Greek play : no mystery about the consequences of Œdipus' action and the curse.

In the modern treatment of the same subject we have versions by Corneille, Dryden, Voltaire, and Chénier. Corneille depended for some of his tragic effects on the existence of an underplot, in which the repercussion of the main theme could be felt. In this he was followed by Dryden and by Voltaire.

Corneille's *Œdipe*, 1657-9, was one of his later and less successful plays. The underplot he uses is the account of the loves of Theseus, King of Athens, and Dircê (daughter of Laius).[1] Here he makes a contrast between a natural and unnatural alliance. Dircê and Theseus in turn attempt to end the plague by sacrificing themselves, but a delay is caused and Œdipus appears as the inheritor of the curse. In Corneille's play the herdman kills himself, and Jocasta, with an economy of properties which is characteristic of

[1] The scene of the coming up of Laius from the shades is recited by Nérine, the confidante. There was no underground machinery on the French stage until Voltaire imitated Elizabethan conditions.

the French stage, uses the same dagger to end her life.[1]
Œdipe is represented as a seventeenth-century stoic, steeling
himself against an evil fate, and ready to deal out the
consequences when he is faced with the facts.

Dryden, though a critic of the French stage, follows
Corneille in the matter of the underplot, the heroine being
Eurydice, not Dircê. In other ways he shows himself to
be affected by the Elizabethan tradition. For example,
he makes Creon a hunchback, like Richard III, from whom
the character is obviously imitated. Creon makes love
to Eurydice and stabs her. Then, again, the ghost of
Laius actually appears on the stage. Finally a very
curiously Elizabethan trait comes out when Œdipus is
pronouncing the curse on the murderer and his children.
Priests confirm the curse, and Jocasta comes in thinking
they are at their devotions. She prays that their prayer
may be fulfilled. Œdipus exclaims that her words have
" fastened " the curse on himself, his family, and nation.

Voltaire at the age of nineteen wrote an *Œdipe* which
was produced in 1718. This play shares with Corneille's
in the idea of an underplot : but in Voltaire's tragedy
Philoctète (formerly in love with Jocaste) appears, and
then disappears leaving the rest of the play to be entirely
Sophoclean. In Voltaire's hands the underplot is used as a
means of arousing sentiment in the audience for Jocaste, who
would have been considered uninteresting unless she could
be shown to harbour a virtuous attachment somewhere.
Jocaste in this play kills herself as a protest against the
injustice of the gods :

" La mort est le seul bien, le seul Dieu qui me reste."
                              " Songez à jamais
Qu'au milieu des horreurs du destin qui m'opprime
J'ai fait rougir les dieux qui m'ont forcée au crime."

There is a touch of realism in the presentation of the
play which is derived from Voltaire's reading of *Macbeth*.
The tragic doubt occurs to Œdipus through the sight of
the drops of human blood on the altar where he makes

---

[1] In Seneca's version Jocasta uses the sword of Œdipus.

his offerings, and through the outbreak of the storm. In Act III Voltaire suggests the existence of the Sophoclean chorus by making Egine allude to the threatening cries of the people, and this suggestion furnishes the atmosphere of presage during four scenes of the act. In this way he obtains a unity of impression. Again, the many references throughout the play to the moral blindness of Œdipe, and the destiny of darkness before him, are intended to prepare the audience for the great catastrophe : though as Voltaire's Œdipe is not blinded on the stage, it is left uncertain whether the punishment is physical as well as moral.

The *Œdipe roi* of Marie-Joseph Chénier is interesting as a contrast to Voltaire's. The language has the rhythmical flow and choice words that we associate with Chénier's writing. But the play is not only a practical rendering into French of Sophocles' drama, it is also a political document. Chénier felt the spirit of the Revolution and he used this play, like *Charles IX* and others, to recall the King of France to his duty as a patriot-king. The threats used by the high priest to Œdipe are changed in view of this context.

"Soyez encore Œdipe, et sauvez vos sujets ;
  Pour nous avec les dieux que la terre conspire ;
  Que bientôt, roi de nom, vous n'aurez plus d'empire . . ." [1]

The people are recalled to their allegiance by the king : [2]

" Ecoutez, retenez, rappelez-vous sans cesse
  Les ordres, les serments, les vœux de votre roi,"

and there is a constant appeal beyond both human law and practice to equity.

In the dialogue between Œdipe and Creon, who is represented as self-sacrificing and self-controlled, Œdipe says :

" Vous désobeissez aux volontés d'un roi ! "

and Creon answers :

" Oui ; son pouvoir n'est rien, séparé de la loi."

[1] Act I, sc 1.
[2] Act I, sc. 2.

10

Finally Œdipe calls on the Thebans, and Creon acquiesces :

" C'est moi qui les appelle ;
Nos libertés, nos jours, ne sont pas votre bien,
Vous êtres roi de Thèbes, et j'en suis citoyen."[1]

In accordance with the classicism of the period there
is no attempt to alter the simplicity of the Greek staging,
and the chorus remains.

There are some other points to notice in all these modern
renderings.

Dryden states that Œdipus and Jocasta have a mysterious
instinct of their filial and maternal relationship. Voltaire
puts it more crudely, and states that Jocasta has a sort of
terror of the conjugal relation. In Corneille's play it is
Oreste who has an instinctive knowledge of his relationship to Dircê. Chénier keeps more closely to Sophocles,
and Jocasta speaks merely of the likeness between Laius
and Œdipus.

Then again, in the matter of Œdipus' encounter with
Laius, Corneille's view is that Œdipus believes Laius to
have been attacked by several robbers. This is rather a
difficult and unlikely point to press. Dryden thinks
Œdipus has known the fact and forgotten it. In Voltaire's
play Œdipe is too polite to question the assertion of others :
while Jocaste really thinks Œdipe's mind was confused
by the action of the gods. Chénier returns to the direct
problem and shows Œdipus' mind seizing on the threads
of evidence and being led logically and without hesitation
to the discovery. As in the Greek play, it is the discovery
that is the crisis.

Corneille and Voltaire did not bring the blinded Œdipus
on to the stage. Voltaire lowered the lights and hid him
in a crowd. Dryden, with his desire for realism, brought
Œdipus on to the stage : and the theatre emptied before
the end of each performance. Chénier recovered the scene
of Œdipus' recognition of his children.

In later representations of the play the sense of archæological exactness allows Œdipus to appear on the stage
when blinded, without injuring modern susceptibilities.

[1] Act III, sc. 2.

The play as acted at Harvard in 1881 was a reproduction and not a version, and as such was both exact and successful. In the same year *Œdipe* was magnificently acted at the " Comédie française," and the mental misery of Œdipe was so strongly shown that the physical horror was the less in evidence. In Reinhardt's version in London in 1912, the German view of the Elizabethan tradition spoiled the last Act and Œdipus trailed the horror with him through the crowd.

(3) ANTIGONE

The development of the idea of moral conflict can be illustrated from the *Antigone*.

Æschylus at the end of the *Seven Against Thebes* causes the herald to say that burial was to be denied to Polynices. Antigone decides to offer the burial rites. In this play the chorus separates into two parts : one half goes with her, and the other half to see the burial of Polynices. Public opinion is divided on the subject of Antigone's action.[1] Sophocles' *Antigone* shows a considerable development from Æschylus' play. The action takes place at Thebes, where Creon is king. His shepherds Eteocles and Polynices have slain one another. Antigone is threatened with death if she buries the corpse of Polynices or offers the formal rite of sprinkling it with earth. Antigone decides to do this, quoting the higher law of the gods, which is the law of family responsibility as against a state edict : Ismene shares the responsibility with her. Hæmon, son of Creon, is betrothed to Antigone. As the plot develops Creon becomes convinced of his error, but he is too late. Antigone has strangled herself with her veil in her living tomb. The concluding words of the play, " Wisdom is the supreme part of happiness," are understood to mean that there are occasions when formal law must yield. The sympathy aroused by the play is entirely with Antigone.

The late eighteenth-century version of the *Antigone* by Alfieri (1783) loses in force by a more complex treatment

---

[1] Later on, in the Middle Ages, right and wrong have their place at different ends of the stage. This is not the case in Greek staging.

Creon is made into the typical Italian tyrant, who sets a trap into which Antigone falls, and convicts her of disobedience. He makes an appeal to her to marry Hæmon and save her life, but this her pride will not allow her to do. Antigone's responsibility is shared with Argeia, Polynices' widow, who comes at night to sprinkle the corpse.

In this play the interest is in the clash of passions rather than in the struggle between the higher and lower law. Thus Alfieri lessens the rôle of the chorus, explaining that soliloquies to help forward action should be put into the mouths of the principal actors, who would naturally give vent to their impulses in words before they came to deeds. The part of expression of a moral opinion, which belongs to the Greek chorus, is entirely omitted by Alfieri. His idea of tragedy is the working out (as in Racine) of human passions in conflict. To the staging he is indifferent. The unities are disregarded so long as the unity of action " which is placed in the heart of man " is kept.

His play has no reference to the fate which overhangs a family, nor to the after-effects of crime. It is simply a human story, in which several actors are temporarily involved. It demands no special scenery, any more than Racine's plays, and was played on a shallow stage with a much ornamented and decorative background. For the purpose of stage-production Alfieri would have cut the Greek story short at the crisis, and omitted all reference to the future.

(4) IPHIGENIA

The use made at different periods of different elements in a central action can be illustrated from the *Iphigenia*. The character and story of Iphigenia appear in Æschylus' *Agamemnon* and in Sophocles' *Electra*. According to the early versions of the history Iphigenia was actually sacrificed at Aulis. According to a later version she was saved by Artemis and became a priestess among the Tauri, where she had the opportunity of saving her brother Orestes from a ritual sacrifice.

Euripides treated both stories. In the *Iphigenia in*

Aulis the chorus alternately speaks the mind of the innocent Iphigenia and of the spectators moved with pity
at the fate of the princess. That fate is engineered by
her father's obedience to a rite of sacrifice. An especially
tragic touch is given by the summons to Iphigenia to
become the bride of Achilles, and by Agamemnon's sinful
consciousness of the wrong he has done his daughter, which
appears in the dialogue and is plain to the audience.
Achilles' ignorance of the rôle assigned to him constitutes
another element of misunderstanding on the stage, one to
which only the audience has the key. Iphigenia's sacrifice
is a voluntary one, and she is rescued by Artemis.

In the French version of the play Racine chooses a
different way of escape for Iphigenia by the introduction
of the character of Eriphile, who becomes the substitute
for Iphigenia. The French dramatist has rationalized
the play, while accepting the conditions of the Greek
legend, by surmounting the difficulties in a natural instead
of a supernatural way. He retains the elements of misunderstanding that we find in Euripides, and the audience
is aware, as in the Greek play, of the double meaning
underlying Agamemnon's speech. Iphigénie is willing to
sacrifice herself, but her life is restored to her as the bride
of Achilles in the earthly life. In Euripides' *Iphigenia
in Tauris*, which was performed about 413 B.C., we have
the conclusion of the Greek legend. Iphigenia is a priestess
among the Tauri, and the chorus consists of captive Greek
women. She recounts the story of her other life in a
monologue which opens the play : and imagines the death
of Orestes as an interpretation of a dream she has had
about her father's house. Euripides makes full use of
the mystification of Orestes when he falls into Iphigenia's
hands to be presented for sacrifice. Both Iphigenia and
Orestes would have suffered at the hands of Troas, the
prince of the Tauri, but for the intervention of Pallas Athena.

It is this play of Euripides which was the inspiration
for Goethe's *Iphigenia auf Tauris*, written in 1787, more
than a century later than Racine's play (1672). Goethe
represents Iphigenie as the ideal woman who among the

Tauri has succeeded in checking the ancient barbarous
habit of human sacrifice, but in revenge for her refusal
to wed him, Troas urges her to prepare for death the two
Greeks who have fallen into his hands.   Here the tragic
element appears very early in the play, as the strangers
are Orestes and Pylades.   Goethe represents his characters
as all moved by an impulse to explain themselves and
thus cut the knot of Destiny.   The audience is not in
possession of facts concealed from the characters, for
Orestes at once reveals his identity, and Iphigenia acquaints
Troas with her desire to escape with her brother.   Confession removes the madness from Orestes' brain, lightens
the scruples of Iphigenie, and wins over Troas.   Even
the entry of the divine-sent Artemis is an answer to the
single-minded aspiration of Iphigenie.   The play presents
little analogy with the Greek original, but is a fine appeal
to human sentiment and an argument for open sincerity
of conduct, and for moral freedom.   From the struggle
with fate in the Greek drama man has advanced to a belief
in reason in the seventeenth century and in moral freedom
in the eighteenth.   The chorus has disappeared from both
later plays : though in Goethe's play Iphigenie's monologues have variety in metre, and in one case a song is
included.   The relation between the life on the stage and
the life of the audience has been drawn close.

(5) THE MEDEA

The subject of the *Medea* is one which has passed
through very remarkable changes in the history of the
drama : including as it does material for the psychology
of jealousy and also an examination of the supernatural
power attributed to Medea.

Euripides' first play, the *Daughters of Pelias*, dealt with
the early history of Medea, the barbarian princess, whom
Jason took with him to Thessaly where his uncle Pelias
was king. Medea, jealous of his daughters, persuaded
them to treat Pelias according to her knowledge of restor-
ing youth to the old. He died miserably, and Medea,
who had counted on recapturing Jason's love, found that
her conduct had turned his love for her to hatred. In

the *Medea*, a later play, Jason is at Corinth with Medea and her two children : and determines to marry the daughter of Creon, and drive away Medea. Medea obtains a delay and then tries all her arts to keep Jason : first by persuasion and then by a feigned submission. Finally she sends the two children with the poisoned robe for her rival, and slays the children with her own sword. The play is remarkable for the gradual rise of emotional intensity to the crisis, and for the use made of the chorus in the last scene, where the women of Corinth all but rush in to save the innocent children but appear to be hindered by Medea's spell, and then fall back to chant the sin and horror of the world : thus lifting the tragedy before them into its place as a part of the general evil brought about by wrongdoing. Euripides' conception of the story was one in which the tragic crime was caused by the acts both of Medea and of Jason, and the double responsibility is allowed for in the play. It was, in this sense, a singularly wide-minded conception.

Seneca represents Medea and Jason as having lived for ten years happily at Corinth before the scheme of Jason's union with Creusa was made. His play opens on the wedding day, when Medea has already reached the crisis of her emotion. She speaks the prologue, cursing Jason, and is interrupted by the chorus singing the marriage hymn for Creusa.

It is characteristic of the Senecan period that Medea's nurse urges stoical calm on her mistress, and that Medea, bereft of love, of wealth, of human support, still feels she has herself and her own courage on which to depend. It is characteristic, too, that Medea rebels against the absolute authority of Creon, and claims a personal right over Jason. Medea shows in turn the frenzy and the cunning of madness : she fastens beforehand on Jason the murders she is about to commit, while Jason tries to treat her with cold reason. She then calls in her occult powers which have lain dormant during the years of happiness, and she intends to murder her own children, because they are Jason's offspring.

In the last scene, where she is slaying the second child, Jason takes the crime to be his own, but Medea rides off in a car drawn by dragons, and Jason calls after her in the blasphemy of despair, urging her to tell high heaven that there are no gods : as was done in Euripides' version.

Médée was Corneille's earliest tragedy and was founded on Seneca's play. It was easy to dismiss the chorus, which had no essential part in Seneca's drama. Corneille also gave up the unity of place, because, as he explained in his *Examen* to the play, he did not consider it suitable that a witch should utter her incantations in a public place. In other ways he attempted to rationalize the plot. Creusa demanded the golden robe as a wedding gift : Jason reluctantly agreed to obtain it, hence Medea's opportunity for poisoning her rival came easily. Médée, in a fine scene with the confidante Nérine, describes herself as the avenger of the gods.

> " Oui, tu vois en moi seule et le fer et la flamme,
>   Et la terre, et la mer, l'enfer, et les cieux,
>   Et le sceptre des rois, et la foudre des dieux." [1]

Longépierre, in 1694, wrote a *Médée* which is psychologically far superior to Corneille's. Here Jason and Medea each have a " confidant," who counsels moderation. Médée, a wronged women, blindly seeking a way out of the " impasse,": appeals at first to Jason's love, and then to his love for their children. It is on hearing that the children are to be taken from her that Médée's desire for revenge overcomes her love for her children, and she murders them.

> "Ils étaient nés de toi, demandes-tu leurs crimes ? " [2]

Longépierre describes Médée's magic powers, which are also psychic and are brought into play by the violence of her emotion.

In the general tone of the play Médée appears as the instrument which punishes a crime against society, but she herself has become degraded through suffering.

[1] Act I, sc. 5.
[2] Act V, sc. 4.

The most recent, and at the same time the most ambitious rendering of the Greek story, was undertaken by Grillparzer between the years 1818 and 1820. It was a time at which the downfall of Napoleon was still fresh in mind, and when in Austria, where Grillparzer wrote, the problem of the existence of tyranny over nations and individuals was hardly yet on its way to a solution.

Grillparzer adopted the form of the trilogy, but, as in Schiller's *Wallenstein*, the first part of Grillparzer's tragedy is in the nature of a prologue in one act. The author of *Das Goldene Vliess* gives in this prologue the explanation of the tragedy of the later parts of the trilogy. Medea's father, Aietes, has broken the most primitive and binding of all laws, the law of hospitality to a guest : and the slaughter of the " Gastfreund " has brought a curse on the family of Aietes. Thus the first part of the play fulfils the function of the first part in a Greek trilogy.

The setting of the story suggests an enveloping influence of fear and superstition, and the play opens, as in Greece, with the rising of incense from the altar : the stage directions provide for a romantic stage-setting, with a view to bringing in to the modern theatre the element of natural scenery which surrounded the Greek theatre. The metre throughout the play is a free metre, imitated from the Greek choric metres, and designed to give effect to the rhythm of emotion in the play. The actors in Grillparzer's *Medea* have the double duty laid on them of developing the story—the rôle of all actors—and also of quickening and directing the emotion of the audience—the rôle of the chorus in Greece. This latter fact explains the considerable use of monologue in the play.[1]

In the second part of the trilogy, *Die Argonauten*, Medea is imprisoned in spirit by the crime of her father. She is the oracle in virtue of her powers of divination, and at the same time the victim, and the predestined aggressor. While in *Der Gastfreund* Medea's strange powers chiefly appear as the instantaneous translation of will into deed,

[1] Cf. the use of monologue for similar reasons in Corneille and Racine.

in *Die Argonauten* they strike Jason as the result of intoxicating physical beauty.

Medea and her father, linked through crime, continually attempt to impose silence or action on each other, but the will is not free in either case. Medea's attempts at the protection of Jason lead to their union and to the apparent lightening of the curse. Her magical powers over life and death are represented as themselves overcome by her love for Jason, who by her help recovers the fleece.

The last part of the trilogy opens in Corinth, and follows well-known lines, except that in the opening scene Medea gives symbolic burial to the fleece and to all her memories of Colchos ; and that Jason attacks Medea's nurse with bitterness because she reminds him of an episode in the past. The effect is to prepare us for the knowledge that the past cannot be destroyed and that the curse holds. The rivalry, from the first moment, between Creusa and Medea, is presented in the first act and develops through the play. Medea is finally represented as maddened by the loss of her children, until her love for them turns to hatred. There is a large amount of moral balance in the play, for the king, even after his daughter's tragic death at the hands of Medea, attempts to do kingly justice. Jason, too, recognizes his own misdeeds, and Medea in the final scene counsels suffering and penitence and realizes that earthly glory is a dream.

The presentation is somewhat marred by an exhibition of Medea's powers of incantation which reminds us of a Germanic fairy story (she wishes a closed chest open, and dowers the golden garment with power to burn Creusa) ; and all through the trilogy there is no clear view about the real meaning of these supernatural powers. They are in turn instinctive, physical, and witch-like, and as in many Germanic dramas dealing with the supernatural, the author uses them in the play as a motive without any convincing effect. The mainspring of the play is a belief in the necessity for justice. This at once removes it from the more nebulous form of the story and gives it the modern appeal which is desired.

APPENDIX II

THE ROOTS OF TRAGEDY

THE question of the appeal of the Tragic drama is one that is chiefly dealt with in books of dramatic theory. From the time of Aristotle to the present day, men have been asked to accept the view of the Greek philosopher that tragedy is efficient in securing the purgation of the passions. No doubt this end may be achieved : a jealous woman may go away wiser and better from a performance of Euripides' *Medea* or Corneille's *Rodogune* ; while Shakespeare's *Othello* may move us in a like manner. A man full of questionings of the spirit may learn from the story of Hamlet how to develop a wiser courage, a performance of *Phèdre* or *Macbeth* may turn our thoughts to psycho-analysis or to the confessional, but still it is not really for the sake of medicine to the soul that we buy tickets for such plays, or for *Œdipus Rex*, *King Lear*, or *Polyeucte*. The possible effect of the play is one thing : the original impulse which takes us to see a tragedy is another. Nor, again, do we go to see a tragedy with a desire to feed on the horrors depicted on the stage. A person with a taste for horror will take a shorter cut to sensation than he could obtain by spending an evening at a classical tragedy. He will frequent the Vieux Colombier, the Chauve Souris, or the Grand Guignol, or he will take his sensation at an even quicker pace in the cinema. The truth is that we do not take doses of pity and terror for moral reasons, nor do we like horrors for their own sake. But something far more deeply implanted in us than all

155

the morality of the civil life, something more normal and human than the desire to gloat over suffering, rouses us to an interest, and even to a pleasure, in a representation of tragic doubt. This impulse has a great deal to do with the experience of the whole human race, and we may perhaps learn more about it by examining certain groups of tragedies to observe their tendencies, before attempting to reach a conclusion.

But let us first dispose of some common errors of thought, and realize in the first place that tragedy appeals to us on broader grounds than that of the tragic end of the central character. Let us recognize the fact that no great tragedies do, as a whole, " end badly." We should not be so strongly moved by a tragedy if that were the case. We may regard the conclusion as inevitable under the circumstances, we may share in the regret for lost opportunities or a lost life, but given the circumstances and the action, we could not wish the end changed, for we know instinctively that the happy ending we may exact in a " feuilleton " would make nonsense of a tragedy. A sacrifice has had to be made for something better worth keeping than life, for honour, or for another's sake. To see the sacrifice consummated is not to see a " bad ending " to the play.

Another error of thought is that which expects the play to be monotonously steeped in disaster. The true tragedy, that which appeals to our deepest instincts, includes many different elements of success or failure. Even though a tragedy may be mainly composed of the darker elements of human life, there is enough of the stuff of normal human life in it to show that the particular plot or story illustrates a danger, or a failure, or a conflict which is significant to the race, and is a warning, perhaps, to every one ; but the play is not written to assert that this is the only truth about our existence on this planet. There is always enough pedestrian life in a tragedy to support a different view, and it is this fact that lies at the root of the desire for dramatic contrast. Shakespeare has his porters and his grave-diggers and his watchmen on the

beat, but—to take one example—the grave-diggers are
not intended to be merely a foil to Hamlet's subtle questionings—they are there to assert a rough proverbial
philosophy of life, and to show that even crime gives
an opportunity for the grave-digger's *métier* and helps
him to support a respectable existence, not devoid of its
own humours. Greek tragedy has its herdsmen and its
choruses of citizens and women, Latin tragedy its messengers,
Spanish drama its brigands and peasants, French classical
tragedy the " confidantes " and faithful followers. These
carry on the life of the city or the country across the
personal tragedy of the hero. Rome survives Cæsar, and
Denmark Hamlet, and Britain Lear.

In another sense, too, the tragic hero has not lost his
life in vain. For when the crisis of the tragedy comes,
Hamlet or Polyeucte dies, or Œdipus goes into exile, or
Antigone is strangled in her veil, the whole emotion of
the spectators goes out to the man or woman who is held
back by death from acting any further part in the play,
for whom the dirge has been said. In that moment the
victim has conquered us, and not even Portia on her
betrothal night compels the feeling of the audience as does
Cordelia on her bier. As a work of art, then, a tragedy
has no " bad ending " even for the central character ;
it has a supreme crisis in which the pain and grief and
active suffering of the victim is suddenly transmitted to
us, and becomes the burden of the onlookers, and thus the
victim is relieved at once of all his mortal agony and striving.
" The rest is silence " was Hamlet's epitaph on himself.

But a still more remarkable thing happens in certain
tragedies. The dead hero begins a new life as an influence,
a fresh factor in the plot, and lives in the play more fully
than before. He can strive no more—can fail no more—
" commedia finita est "—the acts of this life are over,
but a new one has begun in which the whole force of the
hero's character is felt by the other actors, and he is more
potent than when he was treading the boards with them.
Banquo's ghost—probably played by a living actor on the
Shakespearean stage—the ghost of Hamlet's father, the

spirit of Julius Cæsar, the shade of Germanicus in Chénier's
Tibère ; these all dominate the plot of the tragedies when
the living actor has faded into the historic past : and the
satisfaction of the spirits of the mighty dead is one source
of the sense of exaltation which comes to us at the completion of a tragedy.

> " O Julius Cæsar, thou art mighty yet !
> Thy spirit walks abroad and turns our swords
> In our own proper entrails,"

says Brutus [1] in *Julius Cæsar* ; while Lear, who lived to
the end of the play, and outlived his powers, " but usurped
his life," [2] in a dramatic as well as a literal sense.   Apart
from these general facts which arouse tragic emotion in
the onlookers, there are, however, certain characteristics
of tragic drama to which I have already referred, and
for which an explanation must be sought in the history of
human nature, for that has affected the structure of the
plays under discussion.   These may perhaps be called the
roots of tragedy.

I. It is implied in many plays, notably in the Greek
trilogies, that the dead have to be placated on account
of crime unavenged during their lifetime.   This is true
of the story of the House of Atreus in all its developments.
It furnished, too, the motive in *Hamlet*, and therefore
accounts for one type of tragedy.   A tragic hero becomes
the scapegoat for the sins of his family or his age.   Here
we have a conception that is as old as ritual observance
in relation to social crime. [3]   It certainly goes farther back
than the Levitical law, and the model for this type of
play is probably the story of Cain.   Here the murderer
becomes " a fugitive and a vagabond," and is pursued by
avengers.   (The " mark of Cain " is said by Dr. Frazer [4]
to be a protection of the guilty man against the ghostly
vengeance of the slain.)   In the Greek play the Furies

[1] Act V, sc. 3.
[2] Act V, sc. 3.
[3] This point has been worked out by Miss Janet Spens.
See *The Scapegoat in Tragedy*.
[4] *The Golden Bough.*

typify this ghostly vengeance, and finally destroy the descendants of the original criminal. In *Œdipus Rex* the king going forth chastised into exile uses the same words as Cain: " My punishment is greater than I can bear." Shakespeare's *Richard II* is reminiscent of the same idea. Richard II, in the face of his deposition, thinks of himself as a wanderer and an exile :

> " I'll give my jewels for a set of beads,
> My gorgeous palace for a hermitage,
> My gay apparel for an almsman's gown,
> My sceptre for a palmer's walking staff,
> My subjects for a pair of carved saints,
> And my large Kingdom for a little grave,
> A little little grave, an obscure grave :
> Or I'll be buried in the King's highway,
> Some way of common trade, where subjects' feet
> May hourly trample on their sovereign's head :
> For on my heart they tread now whilst I live ;
> And buried once, why not upon my head ? " [1]

The completion of the tragedy occurs when Exton has murdered Richard, and Bolingbroke utters the last words of the play, in which there is an allusion to the Cain *motif* :

> " They love not poison that do poison need,
> Nor do I thee : though I did wish him dead,
> I hate the murderer, love him murdered.
> The guilt of conscience take thou for thy labour,
> But neither my good word nor princely favour ;
> With Cain go wander through shades of night,
> And never show thy head by day nor night.
>
> Lords, I protest, my soul is full of woe,
> That blood should sprinkle me to make me grow,
> Come, mourn with me for that I do lament,
> And put on sullen black incontinent :
> I'll make a voyage to the Holy Land,
> To wash this blood off from my guilty hand :
> March sadly after : grace my mournings here :
> In weeping after this untimely bier." [2]

[1] Act III, sc. 3.
[2] Act V, sc. 5.

In plays such as the above, and also in many of Lope de Vega's, Racine's, and Alfieri's, old recollections of ancestor-worship, old beliefs in the visitation of the sins of the fathers upon the children unto the third and fourth generation, join with the story of Cain in compelling the tragic *dénouement*.

II. Closely allied to the notion of the tragic hero as scape-goat is that in which he appears as the tempest-tossed adventurer, the fool of Fate—mad or seemingly mad—a Hamlet or an Orestes. The parallel has been drawn by Professor Gilbert Murray,[1] whose examination of the origins of this type of tragic hero brings in very remark-able analogies between the traditional Greek and the tradi-tional Danish story. The common elements seem to be the murder of the mother (in the older Danish original) —the madness of the hero, his hatred of women—shown in the *Iphigenia* and also very emphatically in *Hamlet*—the wandering life—the attempted disguises and ruses. Some primitive folk-tale, deeply embedded in human nature, possibly also some symbol of the destruction and return of life in the world, would seem to be responsible for at least one special current of interest in these two plays.[2] In both th˵ ˌagedies the story of Cain is involved, together with the folk-myth of the seasons, and there also appears a conception of woman as Eve, a temptress who has herself succumbed to temptation. Gertrude, in *Hamlet*,

[1] *Hamlet and Orestes : A Study in Traditional Types.*

[2] " In plays like *Hamlet* or the *Agamemnon* or the *Electra* we have certainly fine and flexible character-study, a varied and well-wrought story, a full command of the technical instruments of the poet and the dramatist, but we have also, I suspect, a strange unanalysed vibration below the surface, an under-current of desires and fears and passions, long-slumbering, yet eternally familiar, which have for thousands of years lain near the root of our most intimate emotions and been wrought into the fabric of our most magical dreams. How far into past ages this stream may reach back, I dare not even surmise ; but it sometimes seems as if the power of stirring it or moving with it were one of the last secrets of genius."—*Hamlet and Orestes*, p. 26.

tries to hide, in comfort and luxury and in deceit of mind, from the consequences of her sin. We shall find, in examining other plays, still closer references to the story of the Fall, interwoven with a conception of humanity as battling against some evil and obscure fate, which sometimes takes the form of temptation, sometimes that of the anger of the gods.

III. In one group, to which belong many of Calderon's plays, including *El Alcalde di Zalamea*, among Greek plays the *Antigone*, Shakespeare's *Romeo and Juliet*, *Andromaque* among the French classics, part of the interest to the audience lies in the desire that the adverse fate should be cheated. There is a feeling of adventure when the hero or heroine is in a difficulty from which it seems still possible to escape, and with this the audience may delightedly sympathize. The greatest stimulus may occur when the hero shows that, save for some sudden stroke of fate, he may be able to overcome his adversaries. The narrowness of the margin between success and failure— the mere instant's delay—an unfortunate error—separates the lovers in *Romeo and Juliet*.

" A greater power than we can contradict
Hath thwarted our intents." [1]

Justice and mercy, in the *Antigone*, just fail to overtake the harm done by cruelty. Here it seems to be the incalculable element of fate which turns the story of an active human life, full of promise and serenity, into tragedy, and which so fixes its plot in a tragic mould that no recovery can take place. The messenger came too late to save Antigone, who should not have suffered the supreme punishment for a sinless crime. Othello's new knowledge was too late to save the innocent Desdemona. Such tragedies are impressive because they are true to real experience. Fate finds the weak place in our armour. Which of us has not learned to know a conflict that ended in defeat, or to meet a fate which blocked the way to recovery? Tragedy of this kind is human general experience in a concentrated

[1] Act V, sc. 3.

form. But the experience is not only that of the individual but also that of the race. The perpetual defeat of human aims at the hands of nature and time, the passing of all things into oblivion, is the inevitable crisis of mortal history. Among more modern writers Maeterlinck has used this type of fate-*motif*. It is the tragedy of failure, loss, and forgetfulness.

IV. A fourth group of plays brings in yet another element. The drama of temptation is told (not as a tragedy) in the *Alcestis* of Euripides, but the play contains a drama of resurrection which it is important to notice in any general view of tragedy. In the *Œdipus Rex, Hippolytus*, in *Phèdre*, in *Lear* and *Macbeth* the temptation is either lust of man or woman or lust of power and wealth. And in each case the temptation attacks insidiously through natural human sentiment, through fancy or imagination run riot, through magnified self-love. It is the original sin of the human race to be accessible to temptation. Tragedy, as thus defined, is the destruction of the conscious moral spirit by irresistible racial forces. The interest in earlier plays —such as the *Œdipus Rex* and the *Hippolytus*—is focused on the man. "The woman tempted me." In *Phèdre* it is fastened on the woman. In the Shakespearean drama the man and the woman are both there, as in *Macbeth*, the one as instigator, the other as actor. Such plays go back to the story of the Fall : re-told in all folk epic, such as the Nibelungenlied and the Arthurian Legend. Thus we find replicas of a provocative and sinful Guinevere, of a Lancelot who falls, of a king (Arthur) who is weak and in the earlier form of the story is a penitent ; of magic which in the last resort cannot protect the hero ; there is exile and punishment, there is the travail of the earth to which the warrior is condemned.[1] Through legend and folk-myth, and alongside of nature-myth, the roots of tragedy reach down to the early history of Adamic man.

There is a form of drama, characteristic of the Christian period, and especially of the mediæval stage, in which the Passion of Christ, the Second Adam, is dramatized. Here,

[1] See Miss Weston, *From Ritual to Romance*.

too, the victim is the victor, and the imagination of the onlookers is fired and uplifted as the head of the serpent is bruised, evil is destroyed, and the gates of hell themselves yield to the conquering Christ. The *Alcestis* of Euripides was a fine foreshadowing of the Christian drama, with its note of repentance for wrongdoing, and the hope of a resurrection of the body.

In all tragedies, then, there is a reference to both racial and personal history. The sense of a fall from innocence, of the coming of death into the world, of the invasion of mind by temptation, and the part taken by man, woman, and the tempting spirit, have been expressed in folk-myth and legend as well as in the familiar records of the Hebrew race and in the Hindu drama. Thus it is not surprising to find that the stuff of tragedy, whether early or late, whether pre- or post-Christian, is the same. But into all post-Christian work and into much pre-Christian drama there enters the more assured knowledge that the end of the play is not the end of the whole story, and that good will prevail.

In the production of a tragedy the nature of the play dictates the treatment, which may lean to the realistic or the symbolic method. Thus, in the adaptation of the play to the stage or the stage to the play, a distinction is almost necessarily made between the play that keeps its most ancient legendary meaning, and the play that emphasizes the romantic character of the tragic hero. In either case the events may be completely improbable, and even inconsecutive, when looked at from the point of view of individual human experience : that does not affect the tragic impression. Whatever is assumed as the basis or cause of the tragedy (or indeed of comedy) is accepted by any audience provided that the producer does not, like Richard Wagner or Stephen Phillips, give us a prologue in Olympus and picture the immortal gods or the fates. This removes the play to the region of opera or melodrama, for an attempt is made to stage what lies within no human experience. Speaking quite generally, great tragedy can adapt itself impartially to any

existing stage, and only asks for a background which is
suitable, because not too closely defined : for the stones
of Greece, or the curtains of the Elizabethan stage, or
the effects of refracted light seen in the Moscow Art theatre.
But Romantic drama, emphasizing the distance in experience of the story from present-day human and individual
life, and taking the hero through many thrilling adventures before his fall (if the end is tragic), demands that
the stage shall yield to the exigencies of the story, and
the setting be realistic—that is, as picturesque as the events.
Thus *Lear* and *Romeo and Juliet* and *Hamlet* and Voltaire's
Tancred and *Semiramis* need the help of scenery—not so
Andromaque and the *Agamemnon*.   Each type of tragic
drama brings with it its own atmosphere, or needs one
to be produced, if not by scenery, then by music : hence
the existence of and the excuse for operatic tragedy.

BIBLIOGRAPHY

FOR CHAPTER I

JAMES TURVEY ALLEN : *The Greek Theater of the Fifth Century before Christ.* Californian Press, 1919.
ARISTOTLE : *Poetics.* Ed. Ingram Bywater. Oxford, 1920.
ARISTOTLE : *Poetics.* Ed. D. S. Margoliouth. London, 1911.
ERICH J. A. BETHE: *Prolegomena zur Geschichte des Theaters in Alterthum.* Leipzig, 1896.
LEWIS D. CAMPBELL : *Tragic Drama in Æschylus, Sophocles and Shakespeare.* 1904.
FRANCIS M. CORNFORD : *The Origin of Attic Comedy.* 1914.
W. DÖRPFELD und E. REISCH : *Das Griechische Theater.* Athens, 1896.
RUDOLF GRAF : *Szenische Untersuchungen zu Menander.*
ARTHUR ELAM HAIGH : *The Attic Theatre.* Oxford University Press, 1907.
R. C. JEBB : *Sophocles. Introduction to and text of the Seven Plays.* Cambridge University Press, 1897.
GOTTLIEB E. LESSING : *Leben Sophokles.*
GILBERT MURRAY : *Four Stages of Greek Religion.* 1912.
FREDERICH NIETZSCHE : *The Birth of Tragedy. Eng. Tr.* 1909.
WILLIAM RIDGEWAY : *The Origin of Tragedy.* 1910.
ARTHUR W. VERRALL : *Euripides.* Cambridge, 1894.
MARCUS VITRUVIUS POLLIO (VITRUVIUS) : *De Architectura.* (Printed from the MS. in 1486.)

FOR CHAPTERS II AND III

G. BAPST : *Essai sur l'histoire du Théâtre.* Paris, 1893.
FREDERICK S. BOAS : *University Drama in the Tudor Age.* 1914.
L. P. CAMPBELL : *Scenes and Machines on the English Stage during the Renaissance.* 1923.

E. K. CHAMBERS : *The Mediæval Stage.* Vols. I and II. Oxford Clarendon Press, 1903.

WILHELM CLOETTA : *Beiträge zur Litteratur—Geschichte des Mittelalters und der Renaissance.* 1890–2.

J. W. CUNLIFFE : *Early British Classical Tragedies.* 1912.

J. JUSSERAND : *Le Théâtre en Angleterre.* Paris, 1881.

E. A. G. LAMBORN and G. B. HARRISON : *Shakespeare, the Man and His Stage.* London, 1923.

W. J. LAWRENCE : *The Elizabethan Playhouse.* Stratford-on-Avon, 1912–13.

E. MÂLE : *L'Art Religieux du XII⁰ siècle en France.*

E. MÂLE : *L'Art Religieux du XIII⁰ siècle en France.* Paris, 1898.

E. MÂLE : *La Fin du Moyen Age.* Paris, 1908.

KARL MANTZIUS : *History of Theatrical Art.* 1903.

LES FRÈRES FRANÇOIS et CLAUDE PARFAICT : *Histoire du Théâtre Français.* 1735–49.

R. CROMPTON RHODES : *The Stagery of Shakespeare.* Birmingham, 1922.

E. M. SPEARING : *Elizabethan Translations of Seneca's Tragedies.* Cambridge, 1912.

E. M. SPEARING : *Studley's Translations of Seneca's Agamemnon and Medea.* Louvain, 1913.

CHARLES EDWARD WHITMORE : *The Supernatural in Tragedy.* Cambridge, Mass., 1915.

FOR CHAPTER IV

JOSEPH QUINCEY ADAMS : *Dramatic Records of Sir Henry Herbert.* 1917.

L. B. CAMPBELL : *Scenes and Machines on the English Stage.* 1923.

G. B. GIRALDI CINTHIO : *Discourse on Comedy and Tragedy.* 1554.

PIERRE CORNEILLE : *Discours des Trois Unités.* 1652–8.

DACIER : *La Mise-en-scène à Paris au XVII⁰ siècle* (Paris).

F. H. D'AUBIGNAC (ABBÉ) : *Pratique du Théâtre.* 1657.

JOHN DRYDEN : *Essay of Dramatic Poesy.* 1668.

JOHN DRYDEN : *Defence of an Essay of Dramatic Poesy.* 1668.

GEORGE FARQUHAR : *Discourse upon Comedy.* 1702.

W. J. LAWRENCE : *The Elizabethan Playhouse.* Stratford-on-Avon, 1912–13.

L. WINSTANLEY : *Hamlet and the Scottish Succession.* 1923.

FOR CHAPTER V

H. BERGSON : *Le Rire.* 1900.
SAMUEL CHAPPUZEAU : *Le Théâtre Français.* 1874.
GOTTLIEB E. LESSING : *Hamburgische Dramaturgie.* 1768.
I. LUZÀN : *Poetica.* 1737.
L. PELLISSIER : *The Neo-Classic Movement in Spain during the Eighteenth Century.*
L. RICCOBONI : *Histoire du Théâtre Italien,* etc. Paris, 1728.
R. STACHEL : *Seneca und das Deutsche Renaissance-drama. Palestra.* Vol. 46. Berlin, 1903–6.
D. C. STUART : *Stage Decoration and the Unity of Place in France in the Seventeenth Century. (Modern Philology.)* Vol. X, pp. 393–406. Chicago, 1913.
L. P. THOMAS : *Le Lyrisme et la Préciosité cultistes en Espagne.* 1909.

FOR CHAPTERS VI, VII, VIII

BAKSHY : *The Path of the Modern Russian Stage.*
G. DESJARDINS : Review of Soumet's *Saül, La Muse Française.* 1824.
DENIS DIDEROT : *Entretiens.*
GUIRAUD : Articles in *La Muse Française.* 1824.
VICTOR HUGO : *Préface de Cromwell.* 1827.
GOTTLIEB E. LESSING : *Hamburgische Dramaturgie.* 1768.
PIERRE LE TOURNEUR : *Translation of Shakespeare into French.* 1821.
KARL MANTZIUS : *History of Theatrical Art.* 1903.
J. BRANDER MATTHEWS : *A Study of the Drama.*
LOUIS SEBASTIEN MERCIER : *Du Théâtre.* 1773.
JEAN JACQUES ROUSSEAU : *Lettre à D'Alembert.* 1758.
A. W. SCHLEGEL and J. LUDWIG TIECK : *Translation of Shakespeare into German.* 1797–1833.
C. H. C. WRIGHT : *French Classicism.* 1920.
FRANÇOIS MARIE AROUET (VOLTAIRE) : Prefaces to plays.

CHRONOLOGICAL TABLE OF DRAMATIC AUTHORS MENTIONED IN THE TEXT

Author	*Date*
ÆSCHYLUS	525–456 B.C.
SOPHOCLES	495–406 B.C.
EURIPIDES	480 406 B.C.
ARISTOPHANES	*c.* 448–385 B.C.
MENANDER	342–291 B.C.
LIVIUS ANDRONICUS	*c.* 284–204 B.C.
NÆVIUS, GNÆUS	*c.* 264–194 B.C.
PLAUTUS, M. ACCIUS	*c.* 254–1 to 184 B.C.
TERENCE, AFER PUBLIUS	Flourished *c.* 185 B.C.
SENECA, L. ANNÆUS (younger)	3 B.C.–A.D. 65.
ROSWITHA OF GANDERSHEIM	*c.* A.D. 935–after A.D. 968
AUTHOR OF " SPONSUS "	Twelfth century.
AUTHOR OF " CONVERSION OF ST. PAUL "	Twelfth century.
AUTHOR OF " ADAM "	Twelfth century.
BODEL, JEAN	Second half twelfth century.
RUTEBŒUF	1245–85.
AUTHOR OF " MIRACLES DE NÔTRE DAME "	1340
AUTHOR OF " TRANSFIGURATION " (York Play)	1340–1350
AUTHOR OF CHESTER " JUDGEMENT "	The Chester Plays were printed probably at the beginning of the fifteenth century, but written fifty or sixty years earlier.

169

Author	Date
AUTHOR OF COVENTRY " SLAUGHTER OF THE INNOCENTS "	Later date probably than the Chester, York, and Wakefield Cycles.
AUTHOR OF " EVERYMAN "	Early fifteenth century.
AUTHOR OF " CASTLE OF PERSEVERANCE "	Oldest Morality play. One of the three " Macro " Plays. Middle of fifteenth century.
GRÉBAN, ARNOUD	c. 1450.
AUTHOR OF " MAÎTRE PATHELIN "	c. 1470
SACHS, HANS	1494–1576
HEYWOOD, JOHN	1497?–1580?
GARNIER, ROBERT	c. 1545–c. 1600
AUTHOR OF " VALENCIENNES PASSION "	1547
VIRTUÉS	1550?–1615
KYD, THOMAS	1558–1594
PEELE, GEORGE	1558–1598
LOPE DE VEGA (Lope Felix de Vega Carpio)	1562–1635
MARLOWE, CHRISTOPHER	1564–1593
SHAKESPEARE, WILLIAM	1564–1616
HARDY, ALEXANDRE	1569?–1631
JONSON, BEN	1573–1637
AYRER, JAKOB	?–1605
MARSTON, JOHN	c. 1575–1634
CALDERON (Pedro Calderon de la Barca)	1600–1681
D'AVENANT, SIR WILLIAM	1606–1668
CORNEILLE, PIERRE	1606–1684
MILTON, JOHN	1608–1674
ROTROU, JEAN	1609–1650
ORRERY, ROGER BOYLE, LORD	1621–1679
MOLIÈRE, JEAN-BAPTISTE	1622–1673
DRYDEN, JOHN	1631–1700
QUINAULT, PHILIPPE	1635–1688
ÉTHEREDGE, SIR GEORGE	c. 1635–1691
RACINE, JEAN	1639–1699
WYCHERLEY, WILLIAM	c. 1640–1716
SHADWELL, THOMAS	c. 1642–1692
VANBRUGH, SIR JOHN	1664–1726
LE SAGE, ALAIN-RÉNÉ	1668–1747

Author	Date
CRÉBILLON, PROSPER J. DE	1674–1762
GAY, JOHN	1685–1732
MARIVAUX, PIERRE CARLET DE CHAMBLAIN DE	1688–1763
NIVELLE DE LA CHAUSSÉE	1692–1754
LILLO, GEORGE	1693–1739
VOLTAIRE, FRANÇOIS MARIE AROUET DE	1694–1778
GOLDONI, CARLO	1707–1793
DIDEROT, DENIS	1713–1784
GOLDSMITH, OLIVER	1728–1774
LESSING, GOTTLIEB	1729–1781
BEAUMARCHAIS, PIERRE AUGUSTIN CARON DE	1732–1799
MERCIER, LOUIS-SEBASTIEN	1740–1814
ALFIERI, VITTORIO	1749–1803
GOETHE, JOHANN WOLFGANG	1749–1832
MONTIANO (Augustin de Montiano y Lugando)	Flourished 1750–1765
SHERIDAN, RICHARD BRINSLEY	1751–1816
SCHILLER, JOHANN CHRISTOPH FRIEDRICH	1759–1805
CHÉNIER, MARIE-JOSEPH	1762–1794
PICARD, LOUIS B.	1769–1828
SCRIBE, EUGÈNE	1791–1861
GRILLPARZER, FRANZ	1791–1872
DELAVIGNE, CASIMIR	1793–1843
DE VIGNY, ALFRED	1797–1863
HUGO, VICTOR	1802–1885
DE MUSSET, ALFRED	1810–1857
AUGIER, ÉMILE	1820–1889
IBSEN, HENRIK	1828–1906
HARDY, THOMAS	1840–
PINERO, SIR ARTHUR	1855–
SHAW, GEORGE BERNARD	1856–
BRIEUX, EUGÈNE	1858–
MAETERLINCK, MAURICE	1862–
GALSWORTHY, JOHN	1867–
ROSTAND, EDMUND	1869–
BATAILLE, HENRI	1872–
DRINKWATER, JOHN	1882–

INDEX